On Having a Critical Faith

On Having a
CRITICAL FAITH

Gerd Theissen

SCM PRESS LTD

In memoriam

Philipp Vielhauer, 1914—1977

Translated by John Bowden from the German
Argumente für einen kritischen Glauben,
Theologische Existenz heute no. 202,
© Christian Kaiser Verlag, Munich 1978.

334 01180 9

First published in English 1979
by SCM Press Ltd
58 Bloomsbury Street, London WC1

Phototypeset by Input Typesetting Ltd, London
and printed in Great Britain by
Billing & Sons Ltd, Guildford and Worcester

Contents

Preface

The ideas put forward here have a long history. They go back to my student days, to the time when I was preoccupied with modern criticisms of religion. The answers to these criticisms given by the various theological schools left me dissatisfied; indeed, I found them a bitter disappointment. I kept asking myself: how can theologians go on working, day after day, when they cannot even give a convincing answer to the suspicion that God is an illusion? I resolved either to find an answer of my own or to give up theology altogether. I did find one, and now, some twelve years later, I would like to pass it on. Perhaps others will find it as helpful as I have.

At a later stage, when I was concerned with the sociological and psychological dimensions of New Testament texts, I often got the impression that suppressed anxieties prevented these questions from being tackled openly. There was a feeling that sociology and psychology might destroy faith. I hope that my book will help to remove such fears, not least in order to improve the chances of making a consistent and scientific investigation of our religion. The problems tackled by scientific study of Christianity and the results achieved will be accepted openly only when they are no longer thought to pose a threat to personal identity. Only then will they be looked at unemotionally, without being seen as a danger to the church.

When I began teaching at school and in the university, I came to learn that it is of the utmost importance that a teacher should be open to his pupils; this is essential, if there is to be a satisfactory human relationship between them. Yet this openness is precisely what is lacking in theology, as I have often found to my cost since my student days. Many theologians often know nothing about the real convictions of those with whom they are talking: what they accept, or what they reject. One disillusioned comment which I heard recently was that theologians are no longer concerned with the truth. That I refuse to believe. It would be utter disaster. But I do hope at least that this book will show all my colleagues and students more clearly than is possible in brief seminars and discussions why I still continue to identify myself with our religious traditions, and how far I do, despite the fact that I have become involved in such 'godless' matters as sociology and psychoanalysis. Given the present situation in the church and in theology, it may sound portentous to say so, but I do think that the greatest problem for theology is the question of the truth, and that the hallmark of the theological teacher must be his openness and his honesty.

This book means more to me than all my other writings. I am therefore particularly grateful to all those who made its publication possible: to the editors of *Theologische Existenz heute,* the series in which it first appeared; to the Director of Christian Kaiser Verlag; to all the people I have never met, who work for the publishers and the printers; and especially to my wife. I have often discussed the ideas which I put forward with my wife, and it will be obvious to the reader that she is a psychologist. It will be less evident that I could not have worked out my ideas without her help, and without her readiness to relieve me of so many burdens. This book has been written while she carried on her full-time work at school, where no committed teacher wants to try to get by with doing a minimum, and while I continued my own work as a lecturer in New Testament studies.

I have dedicated the book to the memory of my teacher Philipp Vielhauer. I first put down on paper the basic ideas which it contains about ten years ago, sitting at his desk, while I was looking after his house. More important than that, though, is the fact that when he taught me, he gave me confidence to trust my own thoughts and reflections; had he not done so, this book would never have been written. I shall miss very much his tolerance of new ideas which differed from his own, a tolerance which was rooted in his own independent judgment.

St Augustin, Easter 1978

'Oh, Roderigo, I am filled with love, filled with awe, that is the only reason I mock. Beyond incense, where everything is clear and serene and transparent, revelations begin; in those regions there are no passing moods, Roderigo, as in earthly love: that which is true today is also true tomorrow, and when I am no longer breathing it will still be true without me, without you. Only the sober man has an intimation of the holy; everything else is stuff and nonsense, believe me, not worth staying in.'

Max Frisch, *Don Juan or the Love of Geometry*
translated by Michael Bullock, Methuen 1969, p. 119

I · Three Criticisms of Religion

The arguments put forward here are focussed on one particular question. If we take seriously the problem of historical relativity, the concern for empirical verification, and present-day ideological scepticism, how much of Christianity can really stand up to criticism? In other words, once we stop assuming that Christianity is a privileged tradition, and give up the claim that the truth is contained, once and for all, in one particular tradition, what is left? What is left if we question whether we are competent to say anything at all about areas beyond the realm of potential experience? What is left once we stop playing the defensive trick of declaring our own particular sanctuaries out of bounds to psychological and sociological criticisms, as though these criticisms were concerned only with marginal phenomena and other religions? What is left? Anything at all? Is not everything drawn into the vortex of scepticism? I shall try to argue that something in fact remains. For all its obscenities, illusions and daydreams, I believe that Christianity has an authenticity which can make it supremely significant for human life. Most Christians are not so confident. As a result, they are allergic to historical, empiricist and ideological criticism. They mistrust arguments. They prefer to say that faith is a miracle which defies all argument.

Such mistrust is understandable, and perhaps even justified. People who feel able to accept a tradition only if that tradition can stand up to critical examination may take over a good deal of it, but they will jib at one thing. They will find it impossible that a tradition, an objective entity, should make absolute claims for itself. Anyone who is prepared to argue must inevitably renounce any such claims to absoluteness. He or she may feel able to offer unconditional personal commitment, but will not be able to escape the fact that anything open to argument can always be corrected and superseded. Arguments lead only to relative truths, knowledge of which is conditioned by the historical situation in which we find ourselves. In such a situation, what we are looking for is

1

truth that can be communicated, truth which changes in the course of dialogue. Here, therefore, 'truth' is not a limited number of established propositions; it is rather a demand to put all present and potential statements to the test. Truth is a normative idea. And the nearest we can get to it is always to make sure that our errors are open to correction (which becomes much more difficult when they are shrouded in the mists of absolute claims). But is it possible to think in this way and still to be religious? Is it possible to think in this way and be a Christian? Yes, but only if we are prepared to revise our conception of Christianity.

1. Relativity and historical consciousness

For a long time people believed that the ultimate truth had been revealed once and for all in the New Testament and was now in the hands of a privileged group who passed on the theological tradition. This truth had continually to be adapted afresh to changing historical situations, a task made increasingly more laborious by constant progress in scientific research. No one who is seriously involved in the historical-critical interpretation of inherited traditions can share this view. Historical-critical research inevitably relativizes its subject matter, regardless of any particular results it may produce and regardless of whether these results conflict with the views of the church or not. However it proceeds, historical-critical study must inevitably deny that its subject-matter is the exclusive possession of a privileged group who hand on their tradition. The subject-matter of historical-critical research must be universally accessible. There is no alternative: the demand is intrinsic to both methods and results.

(a) Relativity and the methods of historical criticism

Historical criticism is addressed to anyone capable of understanding it, and not just to a privileged group handing on a particular tradition. By its very nature, historical criticism is concerned to make particular traditions generally accessible. Here it pursues quite different aims from those 'theological' interpretations which begin with the premise that only Christians can legitimately deal with the biblical tradition and anything contrary to Christian views stems from an inappropriate understanding of the tradition. To hold such a view would be as nonsensical as to assert that only Hindus can interpret the Vedas properly, that only Marxists can understand Marx properly, and that only Rilke devotees are called on to interpret his poetry. There is no privileged knowledge in scientific investigation of traditions. Anyone who argues to the contrary betrays the ethos of critical interpretation, which is *ipso facto* concerned with universal communication. It is concerned with understanding, and therefore with breaking down the barriers between people with different cultural backgrounds, different religions or different views of the world. There is no doubt that some people find it easier than others to come to grips with a particular tradition. It is undeniable that Christians and Jews are at an advantage when it comes to understanding the biblical traditions. However, to make this affinity into a norm and to declare that there can only be one legitimate basis for understanding is a very suspicious procedure. Scientific investigation of the traditions of Christianity involves interpreting the Bible in such a way that virtually anyone can understand it, even if he or she is not a Christian. Only an attitude of this kind can command unconditional respect from members of any tradition, and to seek such unconditional respect is hardly an un-Christian concern.

(b) Relativity and the results of historical criticism

There is a second way in which historical criticism is directed to a universal audience. It shows how the religious traditions of mankind are all connected together historically. Christianity was the development of a Jewish heresy, and Judaism was a supreme example of Near Eastern religion. In other words, whereas every historical phenomenon is indeed unique and irreplaceable – and it should be noted that this is true of *any* historical phenomenon, not just Christianity – none is ever to be found in complete isolation. So when historical criticism demonstrates that Christianity emerged as a new phenomenon, it does not set it above the rest of human history. New phenomena are always emerging there. And after all, as a new phenomenon Christianity has some very human features: belief in an imminent end to the world, signs of which are already evident (a very human error); belief in demons and a devil (a very human interpretation of negative experiences); and the dependence of theological thinking on less theological concerns (an all too human characteristic). In short, no matter what the aims of any individual scholar may be, historical criticism shows that religious traditions are very earthly, very relative and very questionable. There is no escaping this recognition.

Someone might object, 'But is not historical interpretation also confronted with the unconditional claim of the texts?' Certainly,

3

but that does not mean that it can accept this claim. Historical criticism makes the claim the object of analysis. It points to analogies, to other instances in which absolute claims are made. It investigates the origin of the claim, showing that the way in which the early church made absolute claims for itself was a development of the ethnocentric views of Judaism. It investigates how this claim functions in small marginal groups, which have to cope with the pressures imposed by the rest of society. Protest as one may, there is no getting round the recognition that historical criticism relativizes every claim to absoluteness. And it does so by explaining such claims in the context of particular historical or social conditions. It makes them relative by submerging them in the ongoing stream of history, which brings change everywhere. Thus anyone who seeks to preserve the Christian faith as it has been for centuries has every reason to mistrust historical criticism. And those who accept historical criticism and its inevitable relativism will have to revise their beliefs. They will have to give different reasons for their appeal to the Christian tradition and will have to relate to it in a different way.

2. Empiricism and truth claims

Christianity has to cope with the objections of empiricism as well as with historical criticism. The empiricist approach requires that no statements shall be made which do not have their basis in experience which can be communicated by one person to another. It does not require that statements should be capable of complete verification through experience – that is not even the case with statements in the natural sciences. It does, however, insist that such statements must be capable of examination and correction in the light of experience. Otherwise, it interprets these statements as the expression of subjective feelings, which command respect as such, but have to be understood as projections if they claim to be accounts of objective data. Not too long ago, 'modern' theology was proud of the way in which it had withdrawn its assertions out of the reach of empirical criticism. Theologians affirmed almost unanimously that in principle it was impossible to ground assertions of faith in the realm of experience. Such statements were based, rather, on the unfathomable mystery of divine revelation, which was not generally accessible. That was to take up an unassailable position, a theology of the 'revealed decision'. This theology comprised a claim to possession of a privileged form of

4

knowledge, by virtue of an inexplicable divine decision, which marked its recipients out from all other men. Such an approach can be called a theology of the 'revealed decision' because in the last resort its point of reference is not a non-derivative human decision, but a revealed divine decision. Arguments are of little use against such a position. What role can they play for someone who sees the miraculous working of the grace of God in the fact that he can be certain of what others suspect to be no more than a human projection? If we ask why some statements and not others, some people and not others, enjoy such a privileged position, we get nowhere. If this kind of theology is consistent, it accepts irrationality as a principle. What is the use of pointing to logical contradictions or doubtful historical assertions? The magnitude of the paradox simply serves to promote the greater glory of God. Indeed, why should God not be so sovereign that he reveals himself even in spurious readings in the New Testament? Why should he not be free to make himself known through error? (Those who would dispute this are said to base their view on an erroneous Greek understanding of the truth.) Such a theology of the revealed decision is irrefutable. However, we should remember that a claim is not necessarily true simply because it cannot be refuted, and that anyone who uses this kind of argument as a means to an end inevitably arouses suspicion. Those who appeal to a theology of the revealed decision rely more on objective authorities, on history, scripture and kerygma, than on their own experience. They believe that these authorities convey a revelation which in the last resort is beyond any possibility of legitimation. The theology of the revealed decision serves as a justification for authority and therefore often looks more like an attempt to provide a rational legitimation for what are put forward as authoritarian claims. No wonder that after a period in the past when it represented a form of protest within the church, it has now become the theology of the church authorities. A traditional approach which has become a mystery to itself can continue to find legitimation on this basis. For why should God not reveal himself through traditions which are incomprehensible to those who hand them on?

However, we must not forget that a claim is not necessarily true simply because it cannot be refuted. To be true, it must be able to stand up to the test of verification: it must be capable of correction or confirmation through being tested against reality. That being so, religion can justify itself to an empirical approach only if there is such a thing as religious experience, in other words, if it is possible

5

to demonstrate aspects of reality which can serve as a basis for religious statements, and are communicable by one person to another. If there is no point of reference for religious statements in the world in which we live, they must necessarily be regarded as projections in which man projects his subjective experience on to objective reality. Thus in any modern controversy, there must be a strong suspicion that religious traditions are in fact mere projections. This point may seldom be brought out into the open by theologians, but nevertheless it haunts all their discussions. It looks, in fact, as though theologians are attempting to exorcise an omnipresent 'ghost' by a collective conspiracy of silence and with the help of an intellectual coma. However, problems are not solved by suppressing them. And as far as I can see, there is only one solution: traditional religious statements must be reformulated in such a way that they can be shown to be the expressions of possible religious experience. This is the only way of taking seriously the suspicion that religious statements may be projections. There is no alternative. If we are to show what elements in religion are still valid, we must think things through to the end. Anything less is evasion.

3. Religion and ideology

(a) Four arguments

Criticisms based on an empirical approach inevitably lead to ideological criticisms. If no objective basis can be found for religious statements and conceptions, why have they not yet died out, despite all predictions to the contrary? Why do they still affect the thoughts of people with widely differing views? Most attempts to provide an explanation seek to 'unmask' religion as a pathological expression of frustration: they either assume that religion provides illusory compensation for suffering undergone, or assert that religion makes frustration tolerable by interpreting it in other terms.

These two assumptions are expressed in both psychological and sociological terms. The psychological argument takes the following form. On the one hand, because of the harshness of the conditions under which they live, people regress to the security which they enjoyed in early childhood. They recreate it by means of fantasies of an omnipotent heavenly father, in order to make a dream-world which will counterbalance their experience of oppression. On the other hand, they accept their experience of reality by dismissing life as an earthly vale of tears, stifling any desire for fulfilment in this world. Thus in psychological terms religion is interpreted partly as regression and partly as resentment.

Sociological criticism of religion follows the same pattern. Sociologists see the religious hope for a new heaven and a new earth as transcendental consolation for the lower classes, who are allowed to 'live out' their protest against oppression by means of religious conceptions, without posing any danger to the ruling class. To this degree religion is illusory wish-fulfilment. Again, the relationship of dependence upon God is interpreted as a transformation of an actual experience of dependence on the unfathomable complexities of the process of production. Thus religion is interpreted on the one hand as an opiate, and on the other as a fetish. There is no need to go into the contradictions between the four different arguments outlined here, which see religion as expressions of regression and resentment, as an opiate and as a fetish. The common factor in all four arguments put forward by psycho-analytical and Marxist criticisms of religion is that they interpret religion as an expression of a deformed and stunted pattern of life. All criticisms made from this perspective are agreed in asserting that the foundation of religion is not to be discovered in the human condition, but in a pathological distortion of human nature as a result of psychological and social conflicts.

(b) Criticism of the effects of religion

Ideological criticism of religion plays a prophetic role in contemporary society. It requires a change in patterns of religious thought and behaviour; it demands conversion. Religion without criticism of this kind is institutionalized deception. The rejection of the arguments of ideological criticism is often simply an expression of the inability and unwillingness of the old Adam to change. Such rejection is, of course, understandable. Ideological criticism is not concerned to change, reform or revolutionize religion. It is concerned to abolish it. It argues not only that this or that religious conception, this or that religious attitude is ideological, but also that religion itself is quite simply a mistaken form of consciousness. Were this assertion meant to imply that all the effects of religion are pathological or ideological, it would be untenable; for although neurotic and ideological religious phenomena may be more numerous than theologians usually allow, religion has undoubted therapeutic effects and shows itself capable of making effective criticisms of society. One might think of the overcoming of existential anxiety in primitive Christianity, liberation from the pangs of conscience in the Reformation, or engagement of human emotion in romantic Christianity. Social protest is given religious expression in primitive Christianity, among the Circumcellions, the Taborites, the Anabaptists, the Quakers, and so on. Religion has positive effects: one need only think of religious poetry from Notker to Böll or of religious music: anyone who classifies Bach or Brahms as an opiate asks to be laughed at. Nor has anyone yet attempted to 'unmask' Gothic cathedrals as pathological products of frustration. Thus religion has both positive and negative effects. No survey of past history allows us to suppose that religion always has only pathological consequences.

We can conclude from this that the question whether religion has an ideological and a neurotic function is predominantly a practical one. The argument put forward by those who would claim religion to be an ideology, that men of sound mind and just societies no longer need religion, can only be settled in practical terms. Let us work for sound minds and social justice! If the critics are right, religion will inevitably fade into the background when our efforts prove successful. The important thing is to make the attempt. The time is in fact long past when it could be claimed that there was a connection between a decline in religious observances and an increase in social justice and mental health. But this 'experiment' has not yet come to an end. And until it does, the argument of ideological criticism can only be dealt with in theoretical terms, by a consideration of previous religious practices. At this point we come up against the positive and negative effects of religion. Greater weight tends to be given to one or the other depending on individual prejudice. It is hardly possible to put forward a conclusive argument.

(c) Criticism of the genesis of religion

Ideological criticism is not just a theory about the effects of religion. It is also a theory about its origin. In so far as it is a genetic theory, it can allow that religion has positive effects, without having to take back its basic criticism of religion. For something that arose out of a blighted life need not necessarily prove to be detrimental in itself. Systems of immunity come into being through illnesses and then serve to protect health. Consequences are independent of their origin. Might it not be possible that religion, too, arose as a result of the distortion of human life without necessarily having a distorting influence in every respect? We must reckon with this possibility. But in that case we cannot be content to counter ideological criticism with an enumeration of the positive effects of religion. We must consider the conditions in which religion originated. However, the question of the genesis of religion can be answered only in theory. We cannot retrospectively alter the conditions in which religion came into being by anything that we do now. Therefore any theoretical discussion of ideological criticism will primarily be a genetic theory of religion.

(d) Ideological criticism and the question of truth

To describe how an idea originates or what consequences it has is not to say anything about its truth. A dream led Kekulé to discover the benzene ring. In it, he had a vision of snakes biting their tails. Psycho-analysts have interpreted the dream in terms of Kekulé's sexual tensions, and have seen the snakes as sexual symbols. Even assuming that they are right – and I am sceptical – this would not amount to much. The decisive point is that the truth of Kekulé's discovery is not affected by the circumstances in which it was made. No matter how it happened, it remains for all time one of the foundations of modern chemistry. The origin and the truth, the genesis and the validity of a notion, are two different things. The same is true of the relationship between the validity and the effects, the truth and the function of an idea. We cannot determine without further ado whether an idea is true or untrue simply by considering its effects. The truth can have ominous practical consequences; falsehood and error can have fruitful effects. Something that works out in everyday life is not necessarily objectively true; there is no pre-established harmony between what is true and what is practical. That tends to be forgotten by those theologians for whom the objective truth of religious symbols has become a problem, and who now proclaim that all that matters is their significance for individual and social life, either by using existentialist interpretation to transform religious symbols into stimuli for individual behaviour or by reformulating the religious dreams of the past as public demands on the present by means of a political interpretation. There is good reason for both approaches. But it is all too easy to forget that some falsehoods are extremely significant in life. Mistakes produce happiness, narrow-mindedness brings satisfaction and illusions foster life. People can fool themselves with claims which seem to bring emancipation. And all this is particularly characteristic of religion. Here above all, however, one finds that intellectual slovenliness which is prepared to play off

9

contemporary relevance as a higher truth against a supposedly less significant objective truth. But only a corrupt awareness of truth is not concerned with a correspondence between subjective trust and objective reality.

4. Summary

In this book I shall attempt to answer the questions posed by ideological criticism, empirical criticism and historical criticism. There can be no question, however, of defending religion in its traditional form; the questions which I shall outline must inevitably leave their mark on religion. Religious belief will have to change if it is still to stand a chance with our thoughtful contemporaries.

I cannot, of course, discuss all the problems of religion; I shall therefore limit myself to three questions which I shall consider in the following order.

Is religion an expression of blighted life or is it part of the human condition? Here I shall offer an answer to the arguments put forward in ideological criticism.

Are religious symbols projections without any real content, or do they point to an experience which can be communicated from one person to another? Here I shall deal with arguments put forward by empirical criticism.

Is the Christian tradition today simply a matter of historical curiosity or can it be the objective basis of a critical religion? This brings up the question of historical relativity.

In examining these questions there can be no recourse to privileged knowledge or authorities. If in a quiet moment one asks whether there is any reason at all for attributing any kind of privileged knowledge (illumination or revelation) to those who are active in the church and in theology, there can be no doubt about the answer. Nowhere is it possible to detect indications of a privileged access to the truth; one can only see indications of the usual statistical distribution of the average and deviations from the average. Besides, very few Christians claim privileged knowledge for themselves. They modestly point to others: the layman to his minister, the minister to his theological teacher, who points to his professor, and so on. The privileged knowledge claimed by theology turns out to be a reliance on authority: everyone seems to believe that even if he himself cannot give a convincing defence of his faith then someone can: whether the man next door, or the institution, or some great figure from the past. So I shall ignore the view that it is possible to have privileged access to the truth. Instead of this I shall look for technical competence, i.e. competence based on a methodical concern with religion – while remaining all the time aware that competence is difficult to define. In some circumstances the outsider is more competent than the specialist. Instead of reliance on authority I shall look for a critical awareness of our own dependence on traditions and assurances which are rooted in society. My own reflections, too, have a definite setting in society, in conversations with sceptical lay-people and other colleagues. They also have their own setting in my own personal life. And they stand in a historical context, in the tradition of liberal Protestantism represented by the names of Lessing, Schleiermacher and Schweitzer, and by all those who have not been put off from making a thorough enquiry into the truth of religious tradition by the protests of the pious or by a ban on entertaining certain thoughts.

II · Religion and Ideological Criticism

1. Is religion pathological?

There is much to suggest that the possibility of religious experience is intrinsic to the human condition and is not confined to those who are abnormal. I shall try to justify this claim by an argument which at first sight may seem rather strange: religious experience is part of human existence because it is based on a specifically human transformation of the behaviour of the animal towards its environment. It has archaic but not pathological elements, though as in all human characteristics, pathological distortions can be found in the background. To understand this argument we must first consider four features of religious experience which present themselves to a purely descriptive phenomenology of religion. I shall therefore discuss, in succession, the characteristics of transcendence, ambivalence, competitiveness and transparency in religious experience.[1]

(a) Transcendence in religious experience

The objects of religious experience transcend the ordinary every-day world. An 'ontological gulf'[2] permeates reality; it separates the sacred from the profane. One might think of the moon by night, the sacred mountain with its numinous aura, the burning bush, the unexpected stillness at the heart of the storm. The holy is always sharply demarcated from the everyday world, whether because evocative features are differentiated from their surroundings by their form, or because intensity of experience transcends the framework of everyday life. The manifestation of the holy is always marked by a note of unconditional significance. Is there here some split in reality which is hostile to life? Does man look for another reality because he is disappointed and humiliated in the everyday reality of his experiences? There is no doubt that this can be the case. But it is not the whole story. There are archaic elements in the split in reality which produces an unconditionally significant 'holy' reality and an everyday reality which by contrast sometimes pales into insignificance. The forms of the holy: the holy stone, tree, mountain, the sun, and also more abstract structures like the order of nature, all have the same characteristics as those signals in the animal world which call forth particular behaviour, namely improbability and simplicity. The fact that forms of this kind speak to us is a legacy from the past. The reality of our environment still has amazing power to trick us. We still keep finding that anything with an improbable and simple structure speaks to us. Signals in the animal world which provoke particular behaviour have developed numinous qualities of appeal. However, they do not speak to us as they speak to animals: they do not trigger off any specific behaviour in us, but a general sense of wonderment, a fascination that evokes the desire to accord with the reality experienced, to respond to it and in so doing to grow beyond our everyday world. We do not know how to respond. Our reactions are not programmed beforehand. We have to develop them for ourselves. All we can sense clearly is that we have been snatched away from the customary experiences of our everyday world. In origin, this transcendence of the 'other reality' is not a compensation for a blight on our life. Rather, it is the opposite: an expression of longing for a fulfilled life, for a heightening of our experience, for more than life. It is the expression of a holy curiosity which reaches out for something beyond everyday dullness, in search of a reality which has yet to be disclosed. Here we are attracted by voices in our environment. Once they had a specific function, but now they are no longer directed towards human survival; instead they help man to interpret his experience, to fulfil it and to heighten it.

(b) The ambivalence of religious experiences

When men are fascinated by a reality which transcends everyday experience, two contrary impulses are combined: feelings of attraction and repulsion. The numinous is profoundly ambivalent. It is encountered as a *mysterium fascinosum et tremendum* (R. Otto). Man senses his own nothingness: 'Woe is me! For I am lost; for I am a man of unclean lips, and I dwell in the midst of a people of unclean lips . . .' (Isa. 6.5). He sinks into the dust. His life seems absurd and valueless. Yet at the same time he is raised above the dust by a beneficent power. An assurance of meaning, significance and value comes over him: 'Rejoice in the Lord always; again I will say, Rejoice' (Phil. 4.4). Thus the other reality encounters him

13

simultaneously as a law which brings death and a gospel which brings life, as judgment and grace, as a hidden God and a divine revelation. Psycho-analytical criticism of religion would derive this ambivalence from the ambivalent attitude rooted in the Oedipus complex, to the father whom one emulates and loves at the same time, fearing his punishment while identifying with his position. The Marxist criticism of religion would point out that religion is both the sigh of the oppressed creature and a consoling opiate. However, the root of the ambivalence of religious experience lies deeper. The recognition that religious experience is the humanization of an archaic heritage leads us to the following conclusion. With animals, every appeal is univocal: it signals encounter or flight, aggression or sexuality; it calls forth a negative or a positive reaction. For human beings, there is no such univocal connection between signals from the environment and behavioural reactions. Man's drives are hardly specialized. Signals from his world prompt both approach and flight, negative and positive reaction; and these contrary impulses bring about a delicate equipoise: holy reverence, the fascination of an overwhelming experience which even a modern man can have in the face of extraordinary beauty. The ambivalent structure of religious experience is thus based on the limited specialization of our drives, and not just on their pathological distortion.

(c) The competitiveness of religious experiences

Not only is religious experience made up of competing tendencies; any one religious experience competes with others. The holy always manifests itself in a variety of forms: numerous gods, powers, holy figures, revealers, devils and demons. The New Testament is familiar with the conception of the fight between the divine and the satanic world and the subjection of all cosmic powers through Christ. The history of religion shows that almost everything has been revered at one time or another as a manifestation of the holy: the sky, the sun, the moon, the stars, trees, men, abstract structures. All these manifestations of the holy possess an undefinable appeal, or rather undefinable appeals. The term must be put in the plural, since we find such a perplexing multiplicity of appeals. The way in which they compete with one another is a fundamental characteristic of religion. In psycho-analytic terms, this would be interpreted as a projection of competing psychological drives and authorities: in the fight against the chaos monster, order represented by the super-ego asserts itself over the chaotic drives of the id and the unconscious. Or, the cosmic Christ who integrates all powers in himself is interpreted as a symbol for the totality of man which integrates unconscious and archaic elements. Marxist criticism of religion sees the competition of numinous appeals in reality as a form of expression of class conflict: the victory of the gods over the demons reflects the mastery of the upper classes over the lower classes. This is especially plausible, since the demons are often the deposed gods of the vanquished and subjected. There can be no doubt that these interpretations, too, have some justification. But here, too, there is a much simpler explanation for everything. Man differs from the animals in being sensitive to more than a few specific signals. He also responds to anything within his field of perception with a striking or evocative form, i.e. to the whole world with its power to obtrude and arouse, to the many competing appeals made by reality. He has to work out a balance between them, by establishing an order of priority, preferring some forms of the holy and rejecting others. Here each culture makes different decisions. And at this point each individual, once he has gone beyond a naive acceptance of his native culture, has to decide for himself. He has to decide which appeal will have the last word for him: erotic magic, the numinous power of organic life forces, the dynamism of history, the individual sufferer. Even today there is no certainty as to our ultimate obligations, as to what we set our heart on. Thus in the last resort the competitiveness of religious appeals is not derived from the competing drives and authorities of personality, class and social level. It results from man's openness to the world, because he is not *a priori* bound to any one manifestation of the holy and is open to competing appeals. Here, too, the human condition proves itself to be a pre-requisite of the possibility of religious experience.

(d) The transparency of religious experience

Religious experience is always based on particular forms, though it suspects that they have more to them than meets the eye. The sacred tree is not itself holy, but the deity who appears in it. The icon is not the object of religious experience, but the figure represented on it. The man Jesus is not the subject of religious experience, but the revealer of God. The specific form of the holy always becomes transparent to something that appears in it while at the same time concealing itself in a mysterious way. Finally, the holy represents aspects of reality in general: the tree is the world tree; the temple is the 'navel' of the world; the man Jesus is the goal and

15

the centre of world history. Each manifestation of the holy discloses a structured universe, becomes transparent to more comprehensive interrelationships and has a symbolic character. How does criticism of religion interpret this transparent quality of religious experience? Psycho-analysis looks behind the religious symbols for the sexual drives of the libido: the connection between the symbol and its mysterious significance is said to be obscure, because the real (sexual) significance of religious symbolism has been suppressed. The Marxist theory of religion thinks in terms of a mystical expression of social relationships: the mystery of the holy family is the earthly family, the mystery of divine decisions is the inscrutability of earthly processes of production.

Thus religious criticism, too, recognizes the phenomenon of the mysterious transparency of religious symbols, but does not find in it the transparency of basic structures of total reality. Instead, it finds an obscurantist account of human, indeed all-too-human phenomena. In so doing it is by no means mistaken. There is, however, a more fundamental anthropological explanation. The specific appeals presented by the reality of his environment do not affect man as a summons to a specific pattern of behaviour; they are an indefinite demand. Man does not know how to respond. He experiences a tension between the concreteness of the holy form and the indefiniteness of the appeal made by it. He interprets this tension by looking for the source of the appeal outside the specific object, i.e., not in the burning bush, but in a mysterious connection which appears in it yet is not identical with it (in an unknown deity). The more consciously he perceives the indeterminate demand, the more strongly he emphasizes the transcendence of the deity over its concrete manifestation. The more clearly he hears the indeterminate voice, the more clearly the prophetic element comes to the fore in religion. For the basic theme of all prophetic criticism of religion is that God is greater than particular manifestations of him, that every specific form of the holy can be superseded, that the indeterminate appeal cannot have its foundation in any perceptible form or image of what is in heaven, on earth and under the earth. Rather, to identify his appeal with specific manifestations is condemned as idolatry. To sum up: the transparency of the holy derives from the human condition, from man's sensitivity towards an indeterminate obligation which transcends all specific forms of the holy.

(e) Summary

Religion is not *a priori* the expression of a distorted form of human life, as many criticisms suppose. In its basic features, it can be understood as the humanization of an archaic relationship to the environment: an animal's habitat is full of signals to which an instinctual structure of needs lends a clarity in behavioural terms. In the case of human beings there is no comparable connection between environment and behaviour. Their drives are less specialized. There is a gulf between the many different appeals in man's environment and the behaviour with which he responds to them. This changes both the character of these appeals and the behaviour adopted in response to them. On the one hand, appeals are no longer exercised by certain specific signals, but through everything that strikes man by virtue of a special form, structure, evocativeness or improbability. On the other hand, the behaviour which is triggered off is no longer specific: the holy occurs as an unspecific imperative. The unconditional character of the appeal is heightened by the fact that two different patterns of behaviour are combined in any encounter with the holy: attraction and repulsion, flight and approach. In the animal world, each of these opposites is associated with a clearly distinct form, whereas in the human world they are both associated with any form of the holy, so that man experiences the holy as being both fascinating and terrifying, as the paradox of the *mysterium fascinosum et tremendum*. Because religion is thus grounded in the human condition it does not follow that ideological criticisms of religion are unjustified. If religion is part of human life, it is affected by all the distortions and deformities of life: its sordidness, its barbarity and its excesses. There is probably no inhuman action which cannot be found in the history of religion. It does, however, make a decisive difference whether one says that religion is an expression of deformed human life or that it shares in life's deformity – and also in its greatness, its value and its worth.

2. Is religion obsolete?

(a) The historicity of religion

If religion is part of human life, then like everything human, it is historical. We saw how the world does not offer mankind any clear motivational stimuli. Man does not know how to behave by nature.

But as he feels drawn towards an environment which gives him relative security, he has to interpret his environment by making social arrangements; only then does the world become his home. Religion is a collective attempt to relate the whole universe to man and by transforming the objective structures of the world into motivations for human behaviour, to make the world a home. In this transformation of the universe into a world which makes sense to mankind, we can find a variety of different tendencies:

Selection: Man, or more precisely, society, must choose some central features from the confusing and competing abundance of appeals. Every culture seizes on certain manifestations of the holy which seem to it to be central. Competing appeals are suppressed, subordinated or made tabu.

Interpretation: The indefinite appeal must in each instance be interpreted as a definite imperative. Ethical and ritual commands must be formulated and made binding, so that human societies can respond to the holy in a way which presents a social obligation.

Intensification: The uncertainty of religiously motivated behaviour – i.e. man's uncertainty generally about how he should behave – has the effect that the holy is intensified into super-evocative, super-powerful forms. It is as though man sought to overcome his uncertainty as to how to behave and give clarity to his motives by intensifying its power. Whenever men look for motivation, they develop super-evocative forms of good and evil, love and hate, the divine and the demonic. Gods and divinities are intensifications of the appeals presented by reality.

Stabilization: The ambivalence of attraction and repulsion, the *fascinosum* and the *tremendum,* requires that conflicting impulses shall be balanced. But the equilibrium will never be a stable one. However, simply by virtue of this it creates a zone of intense watchfulness, a heightening of awareness and a clarification of the senses: religion makes man sensitive to his good fortune as well as to what dismays him, and seeks to bring him stability in the face of extreme experiences. An important means of achieving this is provided by celebrations at regular intervals: liturgies, rites and feasts.

Religion exists only in specific historical religions, i.e. in selected, interpreted, symbolically intensified, more or less stabilized systems of meaning which can take very different forms. As long as the various cultures existed in relatively closed contexts, this presented no problems. Today, however, cultures are open to one another and come into contact with one another. The naivety with which men could inhabit their various religious worlds, as though each religion were the only one, has now disappeared beyond recall.

Two consequences follow from the insight that religion is inevitably historical (and therefore one-sided).

No society can establish a particular religious world for all time. Whereas animals have an established stock of environmental signals, man is always still on the way towards something that will be finally determinative for him. Again and again he leaves behind the established worlds of religion. In the course of the history of religion he chooses an enormous variety of forms of the holy. He rejects them all. His God of today will become his idol tomorrow. His openness to the world does not allow him to find a final resting place anywhere. By nature man is heretical. It is as though he were testing the whole world for elements which had an appeal for him. And this process is always incomplete. The religious disclosure of reality goes on. Man's process of learning about religion is still not at an end. Mankind still continues to articulate new religious experiences, represent them in symbolic form and again and again adapt the symbols to reality. Lessing called this process of learning the 'education of the human race'.[3]

There is also a second insight. Up till now, all religions have undergone historical changes. They have not, however, regarded themselves in historical terms. They have experienced change, but have not given expression to it; it has been a destiny, not a task. Today, though, religions have become aware of their historicity. While they were shaped unconsciously by men in the past, in present circumstances men must quite deliberately take responsibility for their further history. Man has come of age in religion. He can no longer shift his own responsibility on to the voice of the past. He may be anxious about his task, but he can no longer avoid it.

(b) The 'obsoleteness' of religion

Must we not draw even more radical consequences from the historicity of religion? Even if religion is grounded in the human condition, it might represent an obsolete stage in the history of the human race, as Comte believed. Does not the religious disclosure of reality in fact go further? Has not the investigation of reality proved that religion is obsolete? In that case it would be an antiquarian, rather than a pathological phenomenon. Or, to put the point more precisely, it would not have been a pathological phenomenon in earlier times, but would have to be judged differently today: for to regress to stages of development which are over

19

and done with is pathological behaviour, even if these past stages of development need not be thought unhealthy in themselves. Our problem is, therefore, whether there is such a thing as an irreversible process of secularization in which religion is dissolved. Or does religion preserve an attitude to reality which will never be out of date? Here we can begin from the assured fact that modern self-understanding does not favour a religious attitude to reality. Intensive reaction to the power of reality has given way to a more detached, a cooler, a more reflective attitude. Only in exceptional circumstances is there an experience of the oppressive power of reality. It happens only when a journey takes us away from our everyday world, or in an intense erotic experience. But we are always quick to find an explanation for this. We ourselves, we argue, have conferred a numinous force on our environment by projection; in the last resort, it does not determine us, but we determine ourselves. The response to reality is thus fundamentally a monologue, which man erroneously takes to be a dialogue.

But in this respect could not the modern consciousness be the victim of a delusion – a projection of the fundamental concerns of our life on to the cosmos? We want to dominate nature, to excel our fellow men, to be our own masters. Power over nature, over others, over ourselves – these are the basic concerns of modern consciousness. We see everything in the light of this technical, social and cultural quest for power. It dominates our life, guides our thought and determines our attitudes. We cannot do otherwise. Little room is left for a responsive attitude to reality: that seems to be out of date. Anyone who wants only to control himself, other people and other things, anyone who sees this as the goal and the fulfilment of his life, must reject an attitude in which man allows himself to be controlled from outside. It must seem to him that this attitude alienates him from his 'true' life.

The quest for technological power is indispensable for survival. But for that very reason it must not determine our whole life. At one point Max Frisch expresses the suspicion that technology has 'the knack of eliminating the world as resistance so that we don't have to experience'. The technologist subjects nature 'because he can't tolerate it as a partner'.[4] In fact, anything we feel that we can dominate cannot be our partner. And if despite this we allow ourselves to be affected by appeals from outside ourselves, we quickly arouse the suspicion that here are relics of experience from a time when man was still not master of nature, but was dominated by it in a variety of ways.

20

Our social life is governed by a competitive attitude, the aim of which is superiority over our fellow human beings. We worry in case we are at a disadvantage in the distribution of income, power and prestige. The high premium placed on solidarity in action does not contradict that: solidarity is often no more than a compact between a number of people so that they can exercise power more effectively in the struggle for the distribution of goods in society. To this degree, solidarity is no exception to the prevalence of the competitive approach; it represents its consistent implementation. For here solidarity primarily means a common front against others. It is difficult to explain today how an unconditional appeal goes out from every man, regardless of his achievements in the competition in which individuals and social classes are involved. Rather, sensitivity to the unconditional value of every individual is quickly evaluated as resentment; as a devaluation of those who are superior, successful and competent by those who find it hard to get by. The latter believe in the conditional value of every man so that they can assign the same worth to themselves as do their superiors.

Finally, our spiritual climate is also determined by a sublimated quest for power. Our supreme goal is autonomy and self-determination. By this people often mean more than the inescapable demand that the rule of men by men must be broken down. Often they also mean by it the total permeation of our lives by human purpose and human will. The unconscious, the uncontrollable, the emotional, the fate of the body – all this then seems hostile; and a responsive attitude to reality must be taken almost as a betrayal of the ideal of human autonomy. A responsive attitude indeed seeks to be open to an encounter by which it allows itself to be controlled and to which it readily submits. Our modern consciousness, however, orientated on autonomy, has to understand this control exercised by the appeal inherent in reality as unconscious and indirect self-determination. It is self-determination which has not yet reached the level of awareness. The power of the encounter is interpreted as a projection of man's own power, and the appeal to him as an instance of auto-suggestion. Religion is regarded as 'mauvaise foi' (Sartre), in which men interpret what is really a result of their own decisions in terms of an imperative coming from outside.

There can be no doubt that a responsive attitude to reality is in competition with the predominant quest for power in the modern consciousness. Even more, the modern consciousness which is oriented on power can ultimately interpret a responsive attitude to life only as a frustration of a need for power which it constantly suppresses – in accordance with the argument that anyone who is subservient to an alien power has not been able to master it properly. Hence the suspicion is expressed that traditional religious attitudes contain relics of inadequacy in the face of nature, or that failures interpret this world in religious fantasies, or that men who cannot cope with their freedom unburden themselves by means of religious projections directed upon the reality around them. There are areas where such explanations prove inadequate, because religion can unquestionably further positive experiences which can hardly be derived only from frustration, e.g. experiences of grace, love and security. Here a consciousness oriented on power cannot derive the experiences from a reality to which man can only be a response and an echo, finding deep joy and satisfaction by living in accord with it. For its supreme value is self-determination: what autonomous man has brought about by himself must therefore be most valuable. It follows from this that God, the supreme good, must be a projection by means of which man unconsciously determines himself in order to bring fulfilment to his life. The premises of a consciousness oriented on autonomy permit no other conclusions. However, these conclusions are by no means free from contradiction: religion is interpreted on the one hand as a transfiguration of the negative (above all dependence on nature and fate), and on the other hand as man's unconscious creation of positive values. This contradiction cannot be resolved. We can demonstrate this by means of the arguments that religion is an opiate or a fetish. According to the argument that religion is a fetish, in religion man bows down under his real dependence. Religion is an image of this world. According to the thesis that religion is an opiate, on the other hand, in religion he articulates his longing to be free from such dependence. Religion is an alternative to the world.

The same thing is true of the relationship between the theories of regression and resentment: according to the regression theory, religion would be the unbounded realization of infantile wishes; according to the resentment theory it would consist in the sacrifice of human wishes, which for this purpose must be drastically devalued, on the altar of reality.

These tensions in modern criticism of religion are themselves the expression of an ambivalent attitude towards religion. People are quite happy to inherit its positive content, but they refuse to accept it as a gift from outside. This content cannot be 'grace'; it has to be man's own 'work'. Thus the criticism of religion is the inevitable result of a power-oriented modern consciousness which must regard with suspicion every power other than the power which men exert over themselves, others and nature. Once this has been recognized, we will stop complaining that religious sensitivity is so rare both inside and outside the church, indeed that outside the church as well as within, people take delight in old-fashioned 'religious trappings'. It is as impossible to show some of our contemporaries that religion involves a fundamental relationship to reality, and is not just a reaction to frustration or an unconscious piece of self-realization, as it is to show colours to a blind man. And the same is even true of theologians. For many people, the exercise of power by means of religion may be a highly significant driving force. Personal religious experiences prove more of a hindrance here.

(c) The necessity of religion

Anyone who now expects polemic against the will to power which dominates our life will be disappointed. I shall not say anything about the concerns of technology, the competition in achievements and ideas, the struggle for autonomy, which are indispensable parts of our life. If they seem to discredit a responsive attitude to reality, it does not follow that a responsive attitude is hostile to such power drives. On the contrary, a critical religion can integrate them without being dominated by them. Man's search for autonomy finds one of its boldest realizations in 'autogenous training', where people learn to influence their autonomous nervous system, which otherwise escapes the influence of the will. However, this self-control consists above all in the paradox that one ceases to want to control one's body, and surrenders to it, allowing oneself to be controlled by its rhythms, living in accordance with them and relying on one's organism. Here self-control is based on a pattern of deliberately wanting to be 'controlled' by one's body. It is the same everywhere; the technologist must observe and respect the rules of nature; otherwise he will be overwhelmed by the negative side-effects of his interference in nature. The politician – the embodiment of the man obsessed with power – must respect the will of his fellow-men; otherwise his control of them will be volatile or dictatorial. Technical, social and autonomous power are based on respect for nature, one's fellow-men and one's own life. Anyone who acts in response to reality will also understand his activity as a response to the objective structures of reality as a whole. The religious consciousness can integrate the predominant concerns of the present into itself, but it makes them relative.

But can the modern consciousness integrate religious concerns? Can it be at all open towards a responsive attitude to reality, where this attitude runs counter to our need for power? The modern consciousness is not an absolute unity. It has many levels. It comprises many tensions. While it is certainly shaped by a concern for power, it is also characterized by discontent with the omnipresence of a power complex in technical, social and cultural thinking. For example, Marxist social criticism is directed against the fact that in a competitive society everything becomes a commodity: people and things are reduced to their quantifiable market value and their usefulness no longer plays a decisive role. Only one point needs to be criticized here. Such criticism is not radical enough. Do we see the true face of our human and natural surroundings if we think only of their usefulness and make them serve our needs? Have we achieved true human life once things and people regain their true usefulness? Does not our life find fulfilment only when we come upon something that cannot be measured in terms of market value and usefulness and has a value in itself, to which we try to respond with our own life?

There is one thing about which we should be clear: a power-oriented attitude to reality is necessary for survival, but by itself it does not bring happiness. The simple question remains: why are we subjugating nature? For what purpose do we unleash what is often merciless competition? Why do we seek autonomy and self-determination? Man does not live by bread alone. And today that means that he does not live by producing more energy, developing more medicines, making more cars, communicating more knowledge. All this can make sense. Some of it may even be necessary. But it cannot be an end in itself. Drugs are a blessing when they heal and reduce pain; but they can also cause addiction and act as a substitute for necessary human reactions. Competition can stimulate activity, give birth to new ideas, break up established patterns of thinking and so prove generally beneficial, but often it is simply a useless waste of energy. That is obvious. Criticism of the predominant concern for power is as much an element of modern consciousness as the concern itself. Where this criticism is still to be found, there is an openness to religious questions. And where the criticism is justified, there is an objective function for religion: it offers an alternative to the predominant concern for power, another way of relating to reality. Religion has a function in the

24

modern world because it is not modern, and runs contrary to the fundamental concerns of modern consciousness. It is active by offering resistance, not by undergoing assimilation. Of course, that does not mean that everything that is not modern in religion makes sense. Quite the contrary!

Religion is necessary today because it is an answer to the question of the meaning of human life. Thought oriented on power can provide us with instruments by which to realize our aims, but it cannot give life any abiding meaning. One might rightly object that each individual makes sense of his life in a different way. Some people think that life makes sense if they feel at home in a social group; others, if they can live up to the standards they set themselves; yet others, if they are continually stimulated by new experiences and problems; others, finally, if they achieve something which outlasts their efforts, whether this is the production of a garden gnome or of a philosophical treatise. Each person has a different concern: social, normative, explorative or creative.[5] Depending on his particular bent, each person makes one of these concerns central to his life: i.e., it becomes his conscious or unconscious expectation of reality. If his expectation is confirmed, he feels happy and believes that his life is significant, valuable and meaningful. If reality contradicts his expectation, he finds it absurd and meaningless. As no one knows how life will turn out, there is always a degree of anxiety. Will my expectations be fulfilled? Will I be able to achieve what I want to? Will I be happy?

The religious answer to the question of meaning does not add any new element to the concerns which we have already considered. Rather, it is based on a radical change in the relationship between the expectation of meaning and the reality of the environment. This change consists in the fact that we find our life meaningful because it can be a response to the objective content of reality no matter what concerns may emerge elsewhere. For the religious attitude, anything we may do to further these concerns is no more than an echo and reflection of an already existing meaningful reality to which our behaviour is a response. We develop it further, become responsible for it and find that in turn it makes us responsible.

Let me give an illustration of this. A friend has a holiday and goes to the Alps to relax. First of all the alpine scenery is a means to an end. He hopes that it will be a good place for him to unwind and regain strength. But as he stands on his skis and looks out over the virgin snow, he feels an urge not just to make any old curve with his skis, but to make a beautiful curve, the fascinating line of which will do justice to the countryside around. The expectations which he first brought with him pale into insignificance. To put it more exactly, he now feels that his environment has 'expectations' of him. The alpine scenery has ceased to be the means of fulfilling his concern; rather, he and his concern have become part of the landscape. Each has become aware of the other and can complement the other.[6]

The same thing is true of our life. We begin by looking to reality to fulfil our concerns. But when we undergo a religious change, we respond to reality as in the alpine illustration. All at once our own concerns fade and there remains the one concern to do justice to the transitory life of the reality around us, to formulate a response to it and to leave behind a 'beautiful' trace before we have to depart. So long as our own concerns were predominant we were anxious whether our life would be successful, anxious that we might have an all too pathetic role. This anxiety disappears. Or, more accurately, it is replaced by another concern: our central problem now becomes the question how we can do justice to the demands of reality. With our egocentric attitude, can we become an echo and a reflection of the objective meaning that we experience? Are we not much too obstinate? However, in the very act of putting the question we have left behind our ordinary, limited life and it is as though we were seeing reality in the right perspective for the first time.

(d) Summary

We have tried to show that religion is grounded in the human condition. It is part of life itself and does not derive from some unhealthy distortion in social and psychological conflicts. We have also demonstrated that religion is profoundly un-modern, but finds its opportunity in the shortcomings of modernity. It is a necessary expansion, deepening and correction of our power-oriented modern consciousness, which leaves us in the lurch over one question, the meaning of life. Religion today is therefore as meaningful as it has ever been. However, even if we concede that religion is simply a part of human life and not an obsolete form of life, much less a pathologically distorted form, the central question still remains open. Has religious experience a real content? Does the holy have objective reality? On reflection, we might reasonably doubt even the objectivity of our sensory experience. Remember that we perceive only a narrow frequency band of light rays, that we have no

26

organs for perceiving such fundamental phenomena as magnetic fields, radio-active emanations or ultra-violet light. The world that we perceive is structured and 'distorted' from the perspective of our species. Our sensory perception is full of subjective projections: we actively order the sensations that come to us: for example, we distinguish foreground and background, above and below, or we single out significant features. Now if our sensory perception, which is certainly part of our human existence and not an obsolete or pathological form of it, is itself full of one-sidedness and distortion, how much more questionable are all the total interpretations of reality which we come across in the religions, and which go beyond all sensory experience. Are we perhaps fooling ourselves when we think that we are addressed by reality as a whole and must respond to it? Are not many of the 'alpine experiences' of the kind outlined above to be derived from suggestion or from an unusual psychological state of consciousness? However much we may try to root such experiences in the structure of human existence, that does not make them true. It might be that we have inherited an attraction towards illusions as a natural heritage. That is indeed a depressing thought! But who can guarantee that there is a pre-existent harmony between human needs and the truth? Thus empiricist criticism remains valid, even if the objections made by ideological criticism can be rejected. There may be good reason for supposing that religion is not a reflection of the class struggle, an expression of psychological conflict, an obsolete survival from the past. But that does not mean that its symbols accord with reality. We shall therefore have to discuss this question at length in the next chapter.

III · Empiricist Criticism

Empiricist suspicions about religion take the following form. Religion is a matter of projection. It is possible to distinguish two separate aspects: religious conceptions and imperatives, religious symbols and commands. In each case, the argument goes, man reads his subjective experience, thought and will into reality so that his own thought, experience and behaviour may find justification in the light of reality interpreted in this particular way. The question we have to discuss is therefore: Is religion simply a matter of projection? Or is it also 'reflection', the reflection of objective reality?

1. Are religious conceptions projections?

All theories of projection presuppose an empiricist view of the truth. It is only possible to see what is 'mere projection' if we know what the truth might be. By and large empirical criticism agrees that truth claims must have an adequate basis in experienceable reality (though this basis may in fact be left behind), always assuming that the basis is accessible and communicable to other people (though again, there may be limitations to communicating experiences because others are incapable of comprehending them). 'Modern' theologians are often ready to concede that by empiricist criteria their statements are not objective, that they are not based on any kind of experience, much less experience that can be handed on. Theology, it is argued, is concerned with a 'leap of faith' into the dark, an ultimately unverifiable decision which persists in remaining beyond the reach of rational argument. Given such an approach, it is hard to blame any thoughtful person who feels that it would be quite possible to discuss why religious conceptions should be understood as subjective projections. There do not seem to be any comparable reasons why religious conceptions should be supposed to be grounded in an objective reality. On the contrary, the latter claim is based on a dogmatic confession of faith. Faced with the two possibilities, in my opinion anyone who wants to base his decisions on argument will inevitably decide against religion.

It would also make sense to refuse to make up one's mind at all. But that would be a decision against religion. What would be the point of someone saying, 'Things could be otherwise, my decision is not wholly binding'? Is such a vague reservation any good to religion? At best, some people may find it a help in remaining polite, and refraining from objections when traditional religious views are being expressed.

(a) Religious and scientific experience

Now statements can only be tested if the reality to which they relate can be compared with the reality that we experience. Thus for good or ill, we must look for an 'empirical' basis for religious statements. Traditions, authorities and *a priori* ideas can provide interesting stimuli, attract our attention to something. But they can never in any circumstances be a substitute for contact with reality. We must be able to have personal experience of what we are to believe. Here it should be remembered that scientific experience is not the only form of experience that can be tested by reason. For example, aesthetic experience is also grounded in objective structures of reality; contrary to widespread prejudice, it can be and is discussed. Otherwise the theory of art and education in the arts would be nonsense. Of course, there are considerable differences between scientific and religious experience, but both presuppose a contact with reality. Only two of the differences need to be stressed.

First, scientific statements, like religious statements, have only a limited basis in experience. Any generalization goes beyond this basis. It is hard to give reasons for the validity of a generalization on the basis of a limited number of controlled experiments, but the validity of such generalizations is confirmed again and again. It is based on the confidence that nature is the same today as it was yesterday and will be tomorrow, and that it does not contradict itself. By contrast, religious experience is often contradictory. That means that one can always play off one religious experience against another. Religious experience is intrinsically ambivalent. Every experience of meaning is put in question by experiences of meaninglessness. So here too, as in scientific experience, the starting point is a limited one; here too there is an ultimately unjustifiable requirement that the basis chosen be taken as representative of the whole. In contrast to scientific experience, however, this confidence in the meaningfulness of reality must constantly be tested against experiences of meaninglessness.

Secondly, scientific statements are limited to cognitive aspects of their subject matter (i.e. those that can be grasped by the intellect). The object of scientific research may also have emotional and motivational value, but from a scientific perspective this value is irrelevant, at least to begin with. Science makes a cool and ascetic analysis of the universe and its life, but it contributes little towards making the universe and its life a familiar home in which we may feel secure and know how to behave. Science often even comes into conflict with the interpretations of our reality which engage our emotions and our concerns. Science is interested only in the question of truth, and is coy about any other issue. By contrast, the reality dealt with in religious conceptions inescapably comprises emotional and motivational dimensions as well as religious ones. Religious experience cannot leave anyone 'cold'; it changes them, affects them and leaves its mark on their everyday life.

(b) The structure of religious conceptions

Religious conceptions have a symbolic character. They contain images which derive from the everyday world in which we live, but mean something quite different by them. In religious conceptions, the familiar is projected on to the unfamiliar; the well-known is transferred to the unknown. Earthly images serve as metaphors for heaven, and human life as an illustration of divine mysteries. The 'Father' becomes the image of God, the 'Son' becomes the symbol of the revealer. All religious symbolism is more or less anthropomorphic. Man fashions the mysteries of God in accordance with his own image. And just as man has many different aspects, so too do the religious projections which are fashioned in his image; just as we can distinguish biological, sociological and psychological aspects of man, so too we can distinguish biomorphic, sociomorphic and psychomorphic features in religious symbolism.[7]

The biomorphic aspects of religious symbolism are easiest to consider: God, angels and the devil are conceived of in analogy with a human body, to which are added animal-like features such as wings, horses' hooves and tails. It is now conceded that these are not only poetic images, but obsolete poetic images at that.

Secondly, we have the sociomorphic structure of religious symbolism. This comprises the conception of a God who makes a covenant with his people, guides them through history as their king and finally sends his son to overcome their adversaries. The more incomprehensible the actions of the older king become, the more hopes are directed towards his son. Biblical symbolism is sociomorphic through and through. It has always stood apart from biomorphic and technomorphic interpretations of the world; we may recall the rejection of Gnostic genealogies and emanations in the second century AD or the eighteenth-century deistic controversy, which envisaged God as a great clockmaker. Theologians now concede that sociomorphic imagery is poetic imagery, above all when it deals with social relationships between superhuman beings. Even orthodox theologians are readily excused from believing in angels and devils. The mysteries of loving relationships within the Trinity are more tabu. Most decisively of all, the sociomorphic interpretation of the relationship between God and man is retained: prayer, thanksgiving and praise on the one hand and command, promise and consolation on the other are all social interactions which are still emphatically transferred to the relationship between God and man.

A psychomorphic understanding of divine figures is, however, the approach most deeply rooted in the religious consciousness. All deities have plans, purposes and intentions. Negative emotional aspects tend to be 'demythologized': we do not hear much talk of God's anger. But who would go about demythologizing 'the love of God'? Who could imagine God without will, plan and insight? Who could think of him without any divine purpose, without that hallmark which characterizes all psychological phenomena? This psychomorphic anthropomorphism keeps recurring even in the most faded metaphysical formulae. Psychomorphic metaphors are used where Being reveals itself and withdraws itself; where it makes demands or is indifferent; where it seems directed towards mankind.

Religious anthropomorphism always suggests a similarity, if not an exact parallel, between human and non-human reality. On the one hand, human elements are heightened, intensified and transcended in religious symbolism. On the other hand, any thought of equivalence is rejected, and the divine is defined as the wholly other which escapes all anthropomorphic representation. It is infinite, unlimited, uncanny. Yet the very negation of anthropomorphism also presupposes anthropomorphism. So all religious symbolism is anthropomorphic, regardless of whether it goes by the *via eminentiae* or the *via negationis*.

The anthropomorphic reality which religious statements seek to

31

express must be compared with the reality which we experience; this is the only way of testing its truth-content. The central question is: are there structural affinities between non-human and human reality? Only in an actual affinity between the universe and man can there be a justifiable foundation for the anthropomorphism of religious imagery, even if this does not legitimate all religious imagery.

(c) The basis of religious conceptions in experience

I shall argue that objective reality does contain structures of the holy which are akin to human beings, but that it is not a *sine qua non* of religious experience that this should be interpreted in anthropomorphic terms. Such an interpretation presents problems, even if our epistemological situation does not allow any final verdict. It is problematical even in its most sublime form, in which the encounter which lies at the heart of religious experience is said to be purposive. We do not know whether the purpose and destiny of the universe is concerned with man. True, we sense something of this kind in structures that we experience in religion, but we should not necessarily think here of an intention comparable with our own or of a will directed towards us, as though structures which we find miraculous and improbable had been created by a will corresponding to ours. Such an interpretation is suggested by the phenomena. It is not impossible. It has some poetical justification. But we can adopt a religious attitude to reality and appropriate the symbols of traditional religion even without it. Religious experience would also be valid if its discovery of structural affinities between man and his environment were fortuitous, and we could not say any more about them than that. Theologians who claim privileged knowledge will have to go further in their statements. However, those who forgo privileged knowledge can only say that the anthropomorphic interpretation of reality is a poetic account of experiences which could make sense even without an anthropomorphic interpretation.

Nevertheless, I must stress once again that I am not claiming that it is wrong to interpret our environment in terms of some purpose, i.e. to ground it in a superior divine will. I would simply point out that in some cases religious experience can be justified even without such an interpretation.

Religious experience is concerned with affinities between man and his environment. This is already clear from the concentration of modern religion in inter-human relationships. Only in other people do we encounter something that is wholly and utterly akin to us. Only here does our sense of purpose find a complete echo. All other similarities are partial and fragmentary. So concern for the other person rightly stands at the centre of religious experience (even where 'God' is not defined as concern for one's fellow man). However, this concern does not embrace all the manifestations of the holy. Whatever we may understand by 'God', he cannot be conceived of without his being related to the whole universe, the most distant galaxies and the tiniest atomic elements. He would not be God were he not closely connected with the whole of reality, with the history of nature, and with man. Religion seeks to relate man to the whole of reality, not only to our fellowman, even if our neighbour may concern us more than anyone else.

We therefore need a comprehensive concept which will cover both relationships between human beings and experiences of the holy other than in human relationships, experiences which need not necessarily be interpreted in purposive terms. The one that I shall now introduce is that of 'resonance' or 'the experience of resonance'. It refers to the experiences summed up above in terms of a 'responsive attitude to life'. The term 'resonance' has a number of advantages. First of all, there is no suggestion of purpose about it. What I have in mind is the image of a sounding-board which picks up the vibration of a string and amplifies it to produce a clear tone, without it being the actual purpose of the sounding board to produce such resonance. Such a concept implies not only structural affinities which are objectively present, but also their subjective effects. The subjective reaction of the person involved is also taken into account; what we encounter sets off profound vibrations within us. It affects both our emotions and our sense of purpose. Finally, the concept can bring out the inter-changeability of sender and receiver, of passivity and activity: resonance is a relationship between two poles. The movement can start from either pole. On the one side, man shows his longing for resonance in reality. On the other, he is powerfully affected by the structures in reality which are capable of resonance. He wants to respond to them, feels himself moved and put under an obligation by them. He adopts a responsive attitude towards them.

The fascinating similarities between man and his environment which are discovered in experiences of resonance are limited and fragmentary. Something seems to resist them, something that is represented in traditional religious symbolism in terms of a purpose; it is depicted as satanic, demonic; as rejection and hell. This

33

stifling of the experience of resonance, the extinction of it by hostility or indifference, may be termed the experience of absurdity. Absurdity is the refusal of resonance – though 'refusal' should not be interpreted in anthropomorphic terms. The important thing is that every experience of resonance stands out from the background of possible absurdity. Every experience of resonance presupposes an anticipation of expected resonance. The two belong together: experience of the absurd is only possible where the expectation of resonance is disappointed. For 'the absurd is born of this confrontation between the human need and the unreasonable silence of the world'.[8] And just as in any experience of absurdity there is an echo of the disappointed expectation of resonance, so in every experience of resonance there is an echo of the conquest of absurdity, i.e. the awareness that resonance is not normal, but improbable and miraculous.

We can now attempt a first definition of religion: religion is sensitivity towards the resonance and absurdity of reality. Whether it has a chance of being taken seriously by men who are to be taken seriously depends less on smart pastors, modernized hymn-books and a church capable of competing on the cultural market (though all that is important), than on the question whether there is an experience of the holy which is capable of moving life to the very depths and which at the same time can withstand critical examination. However, the experience of the holy that is accessible to us is a matter of being driven to and fro by experiences of resonance and absurdity, being affected by overwhelming meaning and oppressive meaninglessness, by the *mysterium fascinosum et tremendum* of reality.[9]

(d) Religious experience of the natural order: nomological resonance and experience of the absurd

Feelings of resonance and experiences of the absurd take many forms. If we are to make a critical survey of them, it is desirable to begin with experiences of resonance which can be confirmed by science. The natural sciences have stood the test of verification in arguments about the nature of the truth. That is not to claim that scientific experience is religious experience, but rather that phenomena discovered by science can become the object of religious experience, particularly when the structural affinities between man and the universe discovered in this way are not just stored as pieces of knowledge but experienced as significant for human emotions and concerns. They have to develop the quality of appeal, to attract and repel, to radiate security and insecurity, prompting human action and yet setting limits to it. The precondition for this experience is that the structural affinities discovered by science must be experienced from a perspective which is neither detached scientific observation nor a perspective with the ordinary features of everyday life. Science is not religion, but it can confirm aspects of religious experience, as for example its objective side and its cognitive dimension, and that is what we are concerned with here.

In the natural sciences we look for order and regularity, symmetry and harmony, forms of organization and patterns of direction, i.e. for connections which we can understand and classify according to our principles. This search succeeds time and again, most surprisingly where mathematical constructions which have been developed *a priori* can be applied to reality at a secondary stage:

> The most astounding result of modern natural science is the reiterated discovery (quite apart from this or that mathematical formulation of natural processes) that nature, too, is in its essence a fabric of mathematical relations. Put crudely, the mathematics that man projects out of his own consciousness somehow corresponds to a mathematical reality that is external to him, and which indeed his consciousness appears to reflect.[10]

Intellectual patterns produced and constructed by our understanding find a counterpart in reality to an amazing degree. From the most distant galaxies to the tiniest grains of dust, from macrocosmic structures to those fields, symmetries and processes of which matter is made up, we find everywhere a structural affinity between the constructs of the mathematical mind and objective reality. And this experience of resonance is far, far greater than could have been assumed by anyone living five hundred years ago. It is by no means a matter of course: it is improbable and simple: simple, in that complex structures obey universal laws. We may not be forced to see a sense of purpose in these resonances, but there is no reason why we should not do so. It could well be that the similarity between nature and the structures created by our understanding requires the hypothesis of an objective spirit, a creative understanding or an intrinsic purpose within the universe. These could be excessively poetic interpretations of the phenomenon which in an earlier age were called cosmological and teleological proofs for the existence of God. It is accepted that these proofs have now lost their power of conviction, but the

35

phenomenon has remained. And it is no less mysterious and wonderful than before, especially now that our insights into the ordered structure of nature have been deepened and modified. It has become increasingly clear that nature corresponds to a pattern of information which is present everywhere and obeys a central order. Someone might object that such insights are too abstract, too indirect, too 'cool' to move the human heart. This kind of intellectual love of God is accessible only to a few. Because of this, it should be remembered that the nomological sciences are rooted in pre-scientific experiences: in the observation of recurring, ordered and structured elements in the world, and in delight in an already existing order, which can be generally accessible.

Without belief in a regular order of nature, the natural sciences would be meaningless. We accept such order as an *a priori* starting point: we anticipate it in our experimental hypotheses and theoretical considerations. In our preoccupation with the nomological structures of reality, a conversion can take place like conversions characteristic of religious experience. The person who approaches reality with the expectation of resonance, in the hope that it may give him resonance, becomes someone who feels that need to respond with all his thought and action to the abundance of resonance he finds in reality. It is as though all his thought and action were only an echo and a reflection of objective nomological structures. Albert Einstein has given an impressive description of this conversion, this shift of man from active to passive:

> You will hardly find one among the profounder sort of scientific minds without a religious feeling of his own. But it is different from the religiosity of the naive man. For the latter, God is a being from whose care one hopes to benefit and whose punishment one fears; a sublimation of a feeling similar to that of a child for its father, a being to whom one stands, so to speak, in a personal relation, however deeply it may be tinged with awe.
>
> But the scientist is possessed by the sense of universal causation. The future, to him, is every whit as necessary and determined as the past. There is nothing divine about morality; it is a purely human affair. His religious feeling takes the form of a rapturous amazement at the harmony of natural law, which reveals an intelligence of such superiority that, compared with it, all the systematic thinking and acting of human beings is an utterly insignificant reflection. This feeling is the guiding principle of his life and work, in so far as he succeeds in keeping

himself from the shackles of selfish desire. It is beyond question closely akin to that which has possessed the religious geniuses of all ages.[11]

It is not necessary to share Einstein's religious determinism to accept his description of religious experience. Religious experience makes it less important to us whether our questions and needs find resonance in the reality around us. The decisive problem then is how our life can become resonant to the appeal projected by objective reality. Religion begins with conversion to a responsive attitude to life.

This is often misunderstood in modern criticism of religion. One instance is the well-known 'parable of the non-existent gardener', written by Antony Flew. Here talk of God is reduced to absurdity. There is not even a pointer to God in the natural order:

> Once upon a time two explorers came upon a clearing in the jungle. In the clearing were growing many flowers and many weeds. One explorer says, 'Some gardener must tend this plot.' The other disagrees, 'There is no gardener.' So they pitch their tents and set a watch. No gardener is ever seen. 'But perhaps he is an invisible gardener.' So they set up a barbed-wire fence. They electrify it. They patrol it with bloodhounds. But no shrieks ever suggest that some intruder has received a shock. No movements of the wire ever betray an invisible climber. The bloodhounds never give cry. Yet still the Believer is not convinced. 'But there is a gardener, invisible, intangible, insensible to electric shocks, a gardener who has no scent and makes no sound, a gardener who comes secretly to look after the garden which he loves.' At last the Sceptic despairs, 'But what remains of your original assertion? Just how does what you call an invisible, intangible, eternally elusive gardener differ from an imaginary gardener or even from no gardener at all?'[12]

It is impossible to refute either sceptic or believer. However, both are in error. They suppose that they are discussing a religious attitude to reality. They are therefore concerned either to confirm or to refute a religious interpretation. In this respect, both of them are equally irreligious. In the heart of the primaeval forest, they stumble upon an amazing and improbable phenomenon of order in nature, a garden in the jungle. This, however, does not impress them very much. They quite fail to perceive its appeal, to respond to this evidence of order in the way in which they behave. For them, the garden is a subject for discussion; it does not affect their emotions or their concerns. They discuss and experiment. But what would a truly religious person do? He would exclaim, 'What a splendid garden! Let's have a party, to celebrate finding it! Let's celebrate this occasion regularly! And every time we celebrate, let's remember how we found the garden!' That is the way in which cults are founded.

And there could be a further development. The religious person would say, 'We must be careful to preserve this garden and enlarge it. We must not let the jungle win!' That is the way in which ethical codes are formulated. And in earlier times stories would have been told of a gardener who was responsible for keeping the garden in order. This gardener would have been celebrated in festivals, and commands would have been obeyed, giving rise to a myth, an anthropomorphic account of evocative power to be found in the garden. By contrast, we usually have to content ourselves with investigating the structures of the garden and listening to its appeal. But is the myth really so alien to us?

It is important to remember that scientific experience is not in itself the experience of a religious resonance; it only acquires this character through a new perspective on its subject. It becomes an experience of resonance once the technological attitude intrinsic to science is done away with, i.e. where regularities and structural laws are no longer exclusively assessed in terms of how man can use them to control his environment better. Nature has to be seen to be independent of man's uses for it. Exploiting scientific insights for technological ends is by no means the only possible approach. If we are independent of it, the nomological structure of nature can at times come as near to us as other people. Werner Heisenberg has described this experience in a conversation:

> 'Do you believe in a personal God? I know, of course, how difficult it is to attach a clear meaning to this question, but you can probably appreciate its general purport.'
>
> 'May I rephrase your question?', I asked. 'I myself should prefer the following formulation: Can you, or anyone else, reach the central order of things or events, whose existence seems beyond doubt, as directly as you can reach the soul of another human being? I am using the term "soul" quite deliberately so as not to be misunderstood. If you put your question like that, I would say yes. And because my own experiences do

not matter so much, I might go on to remind you of Pascal's famous text, the one he kept sewn in his jacket. It was headed "Fire" and began with these words: "God of Abraham, Isaac and Jacob – not of the philosophers and sages." I hasten to add that, in this particular form, the text does not apply to me.'

'In other words, you think that you can become aware of the central order with the same intensity as of the soul of another person?'

'Perhaps.'

'Why did you use the word "soul" and not simply speak of another person?'

'Precisely because the word "soul" refers to the central order, to the inner core of a being whose outer manifestations may be highly diverse and pass our understanding.'

'I am not sure whether I am completely with you. After all, we must not exaggerate the importance of our own experiences.'[13]

Despite all such nomological resonance, however, in many respects nature remains dumb and impenetrable. Recognizable connections make up only part of it. On the whole, 'blind' chance seems to prevail in both the smallest units and the most complex organizations. Einstein was never willing to accept this. It went against his cosmic sense of religion. Nevertheless, it seems as though this experience of resonance, too, is only limited and fragmentary. The structures of the universe as a whole are hidden from us. So, too, is the interior of nature. The heart of all things escapes us. Few people find that it communicates itself as intuitively and as closely as the personality of other human beings. This is in accordance with pre-scientific experience: 'Perceiving that the world is "dense", sensing to what degree a stone is foreign and irreducible to us, with what intensity nature or a landscape can negate us ... that denseness and that strangeness of the world is the absurd.'[14]

(e) Religious experience with other human beings: experiences of resonance and absurdity in interpretation, society and love

Without question, shared human experience lies at the heart of contemporary religion. That may sound one-sided, but it is not false. The experiences which move and excite us most are with other people. Here, too, I would like to begin with an aspect which is open to scientific control: the understanding people have of one another. This is the essence of all the humane sciences. After that, we shall have to discuss the experience of common action (i.e. an experience bound up with the social sciences). Finally, it will be necessary to point to a central aspect of social behaviour, in which modern man often has religious experiences, even if he has no other dealings with religion: the experience of physical love. To rule this out would be in accord with a long Christian tradition, but it would be dishonest.

All interpretative disciplines are concerned with man's understanding of man as this is communicated by language, works and actions. They develop understanding rooted in the everyday world into an interpretative method, above all where problems are raised by ancient, fragmentary or incomprehensible texts. Understanding here often seems to be an utterly improbable achievement. A text comes to light after many centuries. We recognize that people like us also lived then, with plans which we can follow through, as we see them in their historical context. And in this process the tremendous distance between our time and theirs, between their life and ours, is overcome, and the present strikes a spark from the past. All this is a confirmation of the human longing for hermeneutical resonance without which philological work would be barren and meaningless. Similarly, such work would also be barren and meaningless were it not connected with an unconditional concern for mutual human understanding in the present. Indeed, the interpretative experience of resonance communicated by philology must seem pale and inessential compared with what is experienced directly in the present. I am not thinking here of everyday communication. People can usually understand one another well enough when it comes to necessities. But complete understanding is something so improbable that the moments of completely successful communication stand out from everyday life like fascinating sparks of brightness.

The interpretative experience of resonance is also characterized by that conversion in which spontaneity becomes receptivity, activity becomes passivity. Thus we approach texts which have come down to us with our own questions, but as we read them thoroughly, we are compelled to ask ourselves questions. The same thing happens in our everyday encounters with people. We regularly confront others with our expectations, concerns and interests and are led – often against our will – to understand ourselves in a new way and to change our opinions and our presuppositions.

40

Often we continue to misunderstand. Interpretative resonance stands out from the absurdity of general incomprehensibility, which ranges from a simple failure to pay attention, to disrupted communication which is poisoned by resentment and competition. Many people find that inability to communicate is the severest hindrance in human relationships; and in some experiments aimed at reshaping our relationships, e.g. in the group-dynamics movement or in new forms of community life, there is a truly religious longing for interpretative resonance. The absurdity of being shut in on oneself, of failure to make contact, of isolation, blights life even where in other respects it is full. Interpretative resonance is one of the most important foundations of human happiness. We are all drawn towards a few people with whom we get on well, whose concerns, attitudes and interests find an echo in our own life. However, the greater part of life seems to be dominated by disrupted communications. One need only think of the spectral character of our intellectual controversies. Here one often gets the impression that existentialists, structuralists, dialecticians, systematicians and other bearers of mysteries couched in incomprehensible jargon are talking hopelessly at cross-purposes, so that decisive questions in our life are obscured rather than illuminated.

The experience of resonance between human beings cannot be fully described in terms of mutual understanding. After understanding comes action; after the social experience of resonance comes the experience that men can help to make life more human, indeed that this help is in itself the beginning of a more human life. In the great social crises of modern times this experience of resonance has been developed in a significant way. In these crises it has become clear that solidarity cannot be limited to help given by individuals, but must involve a change in the fundamental presuppositions of our social life. In short, solidarity is connected with the pattern of a society which is structurally distinct from existing society. Although there may be problems in the way of specifying such a pattern, it seems possible to me to give a formal definition on the following lines. There is solidarity in society when all roles and positions have been distributed in such a way that any member can accept any role and be accepted by anyone in any role. We can clarify this by a theoretical experiment. Suppose that we lived in a pre-existent state before our birth and had a complete view of the roles and positions possible in the society into which we would one day be born, but did not know which role we would be assigned; whether it would be high, middle or low; whether we would be born with radiant health or as cripples; whether in this society we would have success or misfortune. If in these circumstances we could approve a society, then we would have a society which displayed solidarity. Even the humblest role would have to be acceptable to anyone. Even the highest role could be acknowledged without envy. Such a model does not seek utopian equality for all men, nor is it pragmatically concerned with the good fortune of the majority. The criterion of such a society would be those who were hard done by, the most unfortunate minority. Even those who were born crippled could live in the awareness that they were respected members of society and that others would not exploit their superiority and strength. The specific form of such a society will inevitably be a matter for dispute. But it will certainly not be identical with the existing form of society and the way in which power, prestige, money and influence are distributed. In any case, longing for a society in which the experience of social resonance is generally possible is one of the most powerful contemporary religious impulses; and this fact cannot be countered by the argument that such a longing often takes repulsively fanatical features. It goes back to a fundamental religious passion, the passion to diminish and remove suffering. It is alive wherever help is given to those who cannot help themselves sufficiently, regardless of whether this is help for individuals or involvement in the struggle on behalf of classes and social groups. Religion cannot possibly flourish where this passion is no longer alive. For every form of religion is measured by the degree to which it contributes to shaping roles in our social life so that everyone can accept his role and be accepted by others in it. In the last resort, the criterion here is not given by those with privileged roles but by the disabled, the stigmatized, the outcast and the oppressed. They are the standard by which we have to measure our social action.

When we apply this standard, the world appears to be profoundly absurd: individual acts of aggression and the collective catastrophes of war; personal experience of injustice and the persecution of whole peoples; the collapse of personal ties and public isolation – all this often makes our world a standing refutation of the longing for resonance. Anyone who recognizes in the picture of a hungry child the web of guilt which binds together all of us who were born with the same right to live but have only fragmentary chances will be irrevocably haunted by the absurdity of our life. This is the gateway to a *mysterium tremendum* in which there are no comforting rites, no extenuating circumstances, no justification, but only contradiction and a refusal to assent, protest and change.

This protest too, however, has its foundation in previous experiences of human solidarity, and it is given duration and permanence by the conversion which is a characteristic of all religious experience. In the egocentricity which comes to them so naturally, people are usually concerned with the question how others can show solidarity with them, how they can be helped in their underprivileged position. But it is often especially useful for us to be as deeply concerned for the suffering of others as we are for our own, for us not to approach our problems in isolation, but together, indeed to subordinate our own life to the appeal of our suffering fellow-humans. The decisive help often lies in a conversion through which everything is seen in a new perspective. This conversion is never final. We keep falling victims to our own natural egocentricity. But what sense would the constantly repeated religious rites and symbols have if they did not keep summoning us to conversion and enabling it to happen to us?

Christianity often had only a broken relationship with the most intensive form of the experience of resonance between human beings. Yet erotic experience has been associated with religion for ages. It has been assessed in either positive or negative terms. But it was never neutral in itself. Only in modern times have there been attempts to make it into a harmless sport. A secularized Puritanism would like to make it a pleasure which involved no conflict. But it will hardly succeed. It will never be able to do away with the erotic fascination which breaks through our everyday life and is certainly not a harmless game. A variety of forms of the experience of resonance are combined in it. They harmonize and together produce a heightened effect. We have here the experience of resonance between living beings, the mutual involvement of two organisms which are flesh of the same flesh (as the Bible puts it). We have an aesthetic experience of resonance which takes delight in the beauty of the human form and in the miracles of the body. We have the experience of interpretative resonance which makes the byplay of love one of the experiences that keeps life going: it gives the natural magic of charm a semiotic character, i.e. it makes charm the sign and expression of acceptance, understanding, value and gratitude. Such interpretative resonance is what gives permanence to fleeting pleasure. Only this makes ecstatic experience radiate into everyday life. Indeed in some cases it can be the foundation for a happy life together even where – say, through

43

illness – lasting happiness in physical love is denied. And here too, in the experience of love, we find that shift of accentuation into the passive which is peculiar to religion. A person may have gone off in search of pleasure at the expense of other people, to satisfy at least his basic needs. But once under the spell of a partner who brings happiness, that person can find an even deeper contentment in responding to the other, putting the other's wishes first, understanding the other's life as an echo of his or her own. Of course, such resonance becomes explicit only at the high points of life: my description is not meant to detract from more harmless contentment. Goethe rightly interpreted this experience in religious terms in his 'Marienbad Elegy', inspired by his meeting with Ulrike von Levetzow:

> The peace of God, which mortals come to know
> beyond all understanding, from above,
> to me seems like that tranquil happy glow
> lit by the presence of the one I love.
> My heart is stilled, and nothing can destroy
> that sense of coming home, that touch of joy.
>
> Within us, pure desire still seeks its goal
> on glorious heights, still faintly earthwards shown,
> would give up gladly body, mind and soul
> before the mystery of the great unknown.
> Holy's our name for such a blessed state,
> which, too, is mine when upon her I wait.
>
> She looks – like springtime's warming sunlight rays;
> She breathes – like breezes rippling banks of bloom;
> and self-regard turns outwards to her gaze,
> freed from the prison of its wintry tomb.
> No petty selfishness with her can stay.
> She comes – and it is vanished clean away.[15]

Of course the suspicion of projection haunts any form of religious experience. Those who are up in the modern social game of psycho-analytical explanation will be ready to mock. Perhaps Goethe may only have imagined that he had been bewitched by Ulrike von Levetzow; in reality he was projecting his ideal youthful self on to her; his religious interpretation of love may really have been a pathological variant of senile eroticism, and so on. However, the most obvious thing is that he was fascinated by the form and nature of this young woman and not by anything else.

44

We ought also to remember that in this encounter Goethe had an experience not only of resonance but also of oppressive absurdity. The failure of his longing, final separation, total estrangement, which casts its shadow over everything, leads him to complain at the end of the 'Marienbad Elegy':

> The world is mine, yet I myself am lost.

Modern philosophy of love lacks this tragic awareness of the possibility of failure. Anyone who makes no mistake is promised pleasure without conflict; and that is why the modern philosophy of love is no less one-sided than the repression of sexual love at other times.

(f) Religious experience of life: organological experience of resonance and absurdity

Before we consider religious experience of life, we must look once again at the difference between the experience of resonance among human beings and nomological resonance. The two forms of religious experience must be clearly distinguished, even if they are associated and kindred experiences of resonance; one is related to the human and one to the extra-human dimension. If we remove the boundaries too quickly, we are left with mythological and technological fantasy. Mythological fantasy emerges when nomological experience of resonance is explained in terms of the model of interpretative resonance, when nature is spoken of as though it were a human partner. When the desire to understand crosses this boundary, as is usual in the case of all metaphysics and religion, what looks like a meaningful text is in fact interpreted as such, though no one has written it. Mythological fantasy arises where interpretations and attitudes which are appropriate in the human sphere are extended beyond it to another sphere where social patterns of speaking, asking, calling and hearing are removed from their original context and transferred to a new context. This mythological fantasy, which can still be found when anyone is engaged in a 'hermeneutic of being', is certainly not an arbitrary interpretation. It is an attractive fantasy, since all experiences of resonance are related and blend into one another; indeed, this fantasy is almost unavoidable, if we are reacting intensively to reality. Yet we must see through it, not to remove it, but to be able to value it as poetry about the holy. As poetry about the holy it has a right to exist, in the same way as the mythology of a sexual

45

encounter between heaven and earth, long discredited, can recur in Eichendorff's poem:

> It was as though the heaven
> had kissed the earth at peace
> which now in drifts of blossom
> dreams deeply without cease.

In the present situation, of course, we need to be warned against the blurring of another boundary. We need to be warned against the unthinking transference of scientific procedures to the human realm. This can give rise to technological fantasy, the delusion that people are and can be determined in the same way as natural processes. This is not, of course, the case. Organisms which solve problems are not mechanical clocks. Much less is man, as he tackles his problems, a cog-wheel in the mechanism of the world (which in any case is much less of a mechanism than used to be thought). He has only a limited capacity to control himself. This is not understood by many social engineers. In contrast, the old myths have something almost humane about them. There, at least, the whole of nature was involved in a drama of social interaction. There everything was socially 'determined'; man was a fellow-agent and partner in all things. Whatever objections must be raised against religious anthropomorphism, at least it humanized the world. It was a naive humanism. Accordingly, we must make a clear distinction between the experience of resonance among human beings and outside them, but we must not separate the two groups. Rather, it is an essential aspect of religious experience that resonance among human beings and apart from them must be taken together. Man does not approach his environment as a stranger; at the same time he is part of it. He is part of nature as an organic living being, as a figure whose beauty can be appreciated, and as one who simply exists. Organological, aesthetic and existential experience of resonance join us to all things. Through them we really become partners in the whole of being. First of all we shall consider the religious experience of life.

Any child knows an elementary experience of resonance when it is attracted by a living creature; for example, when a black bundle proves to be a cat. The time may be past when animals were objects of religious worship, but that deep-seated solidarity with all living creatures has remained which Albert Schweitzer called 'reverence for life', and which was the decisive religious experience for him. He described this experience in a sermon:

What is the difference between a scholar who observes the smallest, unsuspected manifestations of life in a microscope and the old countryman who can hardly read or write, as he stands thoughtfully in his garden watching the blossom bursting out on the branch of a tree? Both are confronted with the riddle of life, and whereas one can describe it more thoroughly than the other, neither will be able to penetrate to the heart of it. All knowledge is in the last resort knowledge of life, and all recognition is astonishment at the riddle of life – reverence for life in its infinite and ever new forms. What does it mean that something should come into being, exist, and pass away? That it should renew itself in other forms of existence, pass away again, emerge again and so on and on, from eternity to eternity? We can do everything and we can do nothing, because for all our wisdom we cannot create anything that lives. What we produce is dead.

Life means strength; it means will coming from a primal source, welling up from it again; it means feeling, sensation, suffering. If you immerse yourself in life, you will look with new eyes into its violent and tumultuous chaos and will suddenly be caught up in it as in a whirlpool. You will rediscover yourself in everything. The beetle lying dead on the road was something that lived, that struggled for its existence as you do. It enjoyed the sun as you do, knew anxiety and sorrow as you do, and now is no more than rotting matter – as you will be one day.

You go outside and it snows. Without thinking, you shake the snow off your sleeves. You happen to look at it; a snowflake shines on your hand. You have to look at it whether you want to or not; it shines out with its miraculous design. Then it quivers. The fine points which give it shape contract, and it is no more. It has melted, died on your hand. The snowflake which fell on to your hand from infinite space and glistened there, has now quivered and died. You are the same. Wherever you see life – there you are.

So what is knowledge, from the most complex to the simplest? Reverence for life, for the incomprehensibility which encounters us in the universe and is like ourselves: different outwardly, yet intrinsically of the same nature as ourselves, fearfully like us, fearfully akin. It is the abolition of the alienation between us and other beings.

Reverence for the infinity of life – removal of alienation – feeling together, suffering together. The final result of knowledge is thus fundamentally the same as that of the commandment of love. Heart and mind agree when we venture to be men who seek to comprehend the depths of things.

And the mind discovers the middle ground between love of God and love of man – love of the creature, reverence for all being, sympathy with all life, however much it may seem to differ outwardly from our own.[16]

Our will-to-live finds resonance in all other wills-to-live: 'As in my will-to-live there is ardent desire for further life and for the mysterious exaltation of the will-to-live which we call pleasure, while there is fear of destruction and of that mysterious depreciation of the will-to-live which we call pain: so too are these in the will-to-live around me, whether it can express itself to me, or remains dumb.'[17] This affinity between our will-to-live and that of all creatures can also be experienced in another way. It is possible to interpret the whole of evolution from aqueous matter to the most complicated organisms as a summons to continue this development towards higher forms of organization: to see it as a heightening of life, as the development of more differentiated forms in art, as the projection of improved insights in science, as the foundation for institutions to safeguard life. In that case, man's own life appears as the echo of an all-embracing tendency of life towards something more than life. Such activity, too, can have its roots in an organological experience of resonance.

Of course, all reverence for life has a tragic dimension. Life must be destroyed for life to be preserved. Deep affinity with all living things turns into horror at their annihilation, at the brutality of devouring and being devoured, exploiting and being exploited. The school of the field, forest and meadow knows little of this. Apart from that, however, has not discussion about the protection of unborn life shown how uncertain we are in our attitude to the sanctity of life, how much we are threatened by inescapable absurdity – regardless of what specific solutions we have preferred for the protection of unborn life?

However, the very vigour of this debate shows to what extent even 'secularized' man is agitated by the experience of organological resonance. In religious experience, too, he undergoes a far-reaching change: identification with others' will-to-live puts his own desire for life in a new light. Our will to intensify our lives, our concern for greater differentiation and awareness, seems to be the echo of an all-embracing will-to-live. And this affinity with all life makes it easier to accept death. Thomas Buddenbrook in Mann's novel puts it like this: 'Where shall I be when I am dead? Ah, it is so brilliantly clear, so overwhelmingly simple! I shall be in all those who have ever, do ever, or ever shall say "I" – especially, however, in all those who say it most fully, potently and gladly!'[18]

(g) Religious experience of the beautiful: aesthetic experience of resonance and absurdity

Aesthetic experience of resonance also comprises resonance between human beings and resonance with the world beyond. On the one hand, art, poetry and music are excellent instances of understanding and interpretative resonance, and on the other hand, in nature beyond the human race there is beauty in the smallest as in the largest things, in visible objects and in abstract structures. It is difficult to conceptualize the effect that aesthetic experiences have on us. We cannot get to the heart of the nature of the world any more than we can get at the heart of our own works of art. Do we know what moves us when we listen to music? Yet it often comes to us as a clear 'revelation', the content of which escapes us should we think that we have deciphered it. For that very reason, aesthetic experience can become religious experience. Wherever we have aesthetic experiences, we perceive in and with their particular object a universal element which seems to reveal itself in the particular. In a spring landscape we may see the eternal renewal of all life; in Othello's jealousy we may see a prime example of captivity to human passions; in the magic of a romantic song the echo of all longing. Often aesthetic experience brings alive in us a side which had been submerged and hidden by the pressure of everyday life; and this experience may be not only cheering and delightful but also eccentric and terrifying. However, aesthetic experience is always open to something that is more than simply aesthetic – which may be gladdening and devastating, pleasant and hateful, meaningful and absurd. Aesthetic experience becomes religious experience wherever it becomes transparent to the abundance of resonance and absurdity in reality, wherever it abandons its primary purpose of being an interruption to work and everyday life and communicates a knowledge of total reality, in such a way that a universal aesthetic transparency becomes a manifestation of the holy.

Of course there is also another element: 'The beautiful seems to have its own independent grace' (Mörike). On the other hand, it could be objected that aesthetic attraction has always been related to particular human needs and has value as entertainment and relaxation; indeed, it even has economic value. Who would dispute that? However, time and again, deeper aesthetic experience compels us to change our attitudes to the beautiful. It forces us to prove ourselves worthy of it. The music lover who deliberately put out his cigarette whenever he was listening to Bach sensed something of this. So did Goethe, when he wrote of the true lover of art: ' . . . he feels that he must rise to the status of artist to enjoy the work; he feels that he must gather himself together from his scattered life, live with the work of art, look at it again and again, and in this way give himself a higher existence.'[19]

Precisely because aesthetic experience cannot compel us to alter our conduct in any way, it can suggest more change to us than we could ever realize. Not, however, by forcing upon us arguments based on particular commitment. Even a completely formal and abstract work of art can communicate to us the vision of a situation in which things regain a value of their own and seem valuable in themselves, without proving useful for our needs.

So the opposite of the experience of aesthetic resonance is not the experience of the hateful. Great art can be hateful. Contemporary art must often be hateful if it is to disclose reality. The aesthetic experience of absurdity consists in the fact that things lose their transparency for total reality, that they are reduced to their banal existence and do not reflect any over-arching connection. The enjoyment of the beautiful becomes an end in itself, in which reality is no longer disclosed, but skilful arrangements ensure that aesthetic attraction stimulates feelings. The experience of aesthetic absurdity consists in the collapse of reality into meaningless individual fragments. The result need not necessarily be hateful and repulsive; as we can see from what appeals to popular taste, it can even take the guise of the choicest treasures.

(h) Religious experience of being: existential experience of resonance and absurdity

The experiences of organological, aesthetic and erotic resonance only partially bridge the divide between resonance among humans and resonance with the non-human world. Life is only a part of total reality, a superficial phenomenon on one planet (or perhaps more); the beautiful captivates us as a fascinating game, but it remains a game, a fantasy in which we need not join. Love can put the world in a new light and fill us with a sensitivity to the sisterly character of all being; but that seems to be the rare exception. This

50

makes all the more urgent the question whether there is an all-embracing experience of resonance which has universal relevance: a fundamental religious experience. This basic experience need not be discredited because it is constantly veiled in obscurity. It is really very simple. It consists in amazement that anything exists at all. This amazement does not address our understanding in its search for nomological structures; here there is no being 'to understand', as the peddlers of ontological mysteries keep telling us. There is no beauty and no life. Rather, our existence sets before us the simple fact that we exist at all. The accidental character of our own existence resonates with the accidental character of all things; the mystery of being finds an echo in the riddle of our individual and contingent existence. This existential resonance can be found in all religious experiences; it connects nomological, interpretative, organological and aesthetic experiences of the holy. For even those things that have a regular structure: life, beauty, have a contingent existence; and even resonance between human beings always involves astonishment, gratitude that the other person exists at all and that one may exist in his or her presence.

Existential resonance is set against the constant presence of a dark background; glad amazement that anything exists at all soon becomes dread at the chance nature of all things. Similarly, a feeling of gratitude for one's own existence is soon darkened by anxiety at being in the world. What makes us happy simultaneously casts us out into a boundless wilderness; what exalts us simultaneously conjures up in us a loathing of all things, so that everything seems absurd and meaningless.

When it finds an echo in us, the contingency of all things is always more than the backlash from an encounter in which we know that we are not involved. When we really become aware of it, we feel that our questions and thoughts about it, our language, our breathing, our very existence, are contingent. It seems as though we forfeit ourselves as subjects who can have an existence independent of what we encounter. What we think that we encounter surrounds us and holds us in its grasp. We find it impossible to speak of it in a detached way; for in it we live and move and have our being. We can come to some intellectual understanding of this 'conversion' by remembering the impossibility of solving the metaphysical problem of the first cause. If we begin with the question 'Why is there anything at all?', we are referred back from one thing to another. Each answer makes us repeat the question on and on in an endless chain. We cannot answer it anyway, since we can always put the same question, 'Why?', to the last link of the chain, though this may be God, or even more than God. The question only finds an answer when it is no longer put, not because there is a refusal to answer it, but because it becomes a question about ourselves. Existence of any kind proves to be a wonder and a mystery; the question of existence proves to be a satisfying or a shattering experience; and being is experienced as value in itself. Our original question was not wrong, but the answer to it cannot be found in any object. The question has to be changed, so that we no longer ask ourselves 'How can we derive the mystery of existence from this or that?', but, 'Can our existence respond to the mystery of being?'

(i) Religious experience and the understanding of God

We began with the question, 'How far can religious conceptions be based on verifiable experiences?' Our answer was: In so far as religious symbols express a structural affinity between man and his environment and indicate its limits, they can be confirmed by religious experience, i.e. by experiences of resonance and absurdity. Religious conceptions have an empirical basis (if we use the term 'empirical' in the wider sense). A representative of a traditional form of religion would now object that religious symbols go far beyond human exerience. Above all, the central symbol 'God' means far more than can be disclosed through religious experience. This objection is justified. What we can experience of God is probably only his shadow, a trace of him in the reality around us. We do not know. We can only decipher what is given. However, what is given points beyond itself. Religious experience is not closed in on itself; it is open.

To sum up once again: we have recognized many forms of religious experience. We have seen that anything that has structure and form, anything that is alive and comprehensible, anything that exists, can evoke profound responses from us: we feel addressed and encountered. The holy takes many forms. It cannot be confined to one. It is potential everywhere. Anything can be its medium: a stone, noonday silence, a passer-by, a conversation, an insight – anything. For example, Buddha saw a beggar, a sick man, a corpse, and this radically changed his life. Albert Schweitzer experienced his success as an obligation to lessen the suffering of others. The omnipresence of holiness (its ubiquity) makes the search for particular starting points for the experience of the holy seem pointless. There is no place where man could find it with any certainty. There is no place where he is safe from it, even if he 'flees to the underworld or ascends to heaven'. He can do only one thing: be open to the call that can come to him at any time; that usually finds him where he does not expect it. This openness of the experience of the holy can be seen elsewhere than in the individual human life. There is also evidence of it throughout the history of religion. The experience of the holy changes with each generation. Each generation is inclined to absolutize a particular form of the holy. Each seeks to limit its potential omnipresence. Such absolutizations can easily be seen today in paraphrases for what used to be called 'God'. God, it is said, is Being itself; God is the order and harmony of nature, the origin of life, human fellowship and love. But if we are to do justice to what has been called God from time immemorial, we ought rather to define God as the inexhaustible abundance of resonances in reality; as an abundance which is possibly undisclosed and unrealized; which perhaps remains undisclosed and unrealized; which time and again stands out against the dark background of possible absurdity. It is useless to look for the holy in a particular object or area. It is not an object alongside other objects, but rather a field made up from all reality – including man; it is comparable to a magnetic field, which can only be perceived once it exerts its force. No limits can be set to it; it is a process which has yet to reach an end. It can never be finally defined and delimited, because no one knows the forms in which man will experience resonance and absurdity in the future. Thus the experience of the holy is open. It points beyond itself.

Consequently we can agree with the objection made by conservative religion. God is more than the field of resonance and absurdity in reality. There is a distinction here, but not a contradiction. The field of resonance and absurdity in reality is what we can experience of God, what Paul calls the *gnoston tou theou* (Rom. 1.19). We call what we experience 'the holy'. Anything beyond that can no longer be experienced; it can only be guessed at. Religious aspirations reach out into a dark area which cannot be covered by religious experience.

Is not this the final point at which we must capitulate with our concern to test religious conceptions by argument? Do we not find ourselves here in the realm of irrational assertions? First of all it should be remembered that here we enter the realm of religious poetry. What we suspect in and behind our religious experiences is shaped by poetic symbols. These symbols cannot be given an adequate foundation by argument alone. We can, however, explain

53

why it is impossible to give them any grounding in argument here. We can explain why they are not to be derived from generally accessible religious experience. Or, to put the argument in a more complicated way: the symbols of religious aspiration are irrational in terms of objective linguistic signification, but it is possible to give a reasonably rational account of the meta-linguistic theory behind them. This can be illustrated by three poetic statements about God, statements which are based on religious aspiration and not experience. These are the symbols of the omnipotence, the personhood and the lordship of God.

The symbol of omnipotence indicates that God is in control of everything. It is rooted in religious experience, since religious experience brings us into a relationship with reality as a whole and calls forth in us the intimation of an all-controlling reality which determines everything from the most distant galaxies to the smallest micro-processes.

By definition, this all-controlling reality can only be guessed at, and cannot be experienced. We can only establish the existence of a factor that controls reality if its influence varies and is sometimes greater, sometimes lesser, or in some conditions disappears altogether. An illustration may perhaps make this clear. If we assumed that air was an all-controlling factor, we could demonstrate this only through reducing or excluding its effects by a vacuum pump. In that event we could then, for example, establish that no growth is possible without air. However, it is inconceivable that we should have a comparable vacuum pump for God. The symbol of omnipotence means that he can never be cut off. So he cannot be experienced. A factor which constantly has the same effect on everything is not susceptible to empirical demonstration. It can only be eliminated roughly, in theoretical terms. Without God, all being would fall back into nothingness. But we would not be able to experience him.

The symbol of the person indicates that God is a power which addresses man and puts him under an obligation. This symbol, too, is rooted in religious experience. The holy comes as near to us in it as the person of another human being, and we intimate behind it a superior person, without being able to experience him directly. If we take the symbol seriously, it puts limits on the general possibility of experiencing God. Whereas things are indifferent as to whether or not they are known, people can disclose themselves or evade notice. If we want to share in their world, they must come out of themselves and disclose themselves to us. We are invited to

54

meet them. Another person's disclosure of him or herself is always a gift. If the symbol of person can be applied to God, he cannot be experienced generally. He can only be guessed at. And without doubt this is the case: many impressions force us to the intimation that the heart of reality is profoundly akin to us. But we cannot experience the heart of reality. Were it known to us, we might see our personhood reflected in it. Perhaps all experiences of resonance would be revealed to us as the answer to a creative and omnipotent personality. But in that case we would perhaps recognize even more how problematical is that personhood which we naively presuppose in ourselves and make the centre of an interpretation of the world. We would have a disclosure not only of the heart of reality, but also of something that hitherto had remained unknown to us: our own personhood, a completely different element. What is the 'I' which has its home in us somewhere between syntax and physiology? Do we know it? Did not it too emerge from a complex organization of elementary particles and fields of energy? Is it something completely different from the rest of reality? Could not the heart of reality be profoundly akin to us and yet differ from that self-conscious personality which we read into reality in religious projections? We do not know what God is in himself. We will never know. But the way in which we experience him is evidently bound up with the way in which we experience ourselves. However, precisely when we are engaged in introspection and in meditative experience, we become aware how much we have overestimated our ego. It is made relative as the instrument of our self-assertion. It loses its paramount significance. So on the basis of meditative experience, too, we can keep open the old question as to whether God is a person. For our own personhood is itself deeper than we suspected.

The symbol of lordship indicates that God is infinitely superior. It is rooted in the religious experience of the overwhelming force with which the whole of reality requires our response. We sense a superior power in the depths of the world. But if we take the symbol of lordship seriously, *a priori* we must reckon with limitations to the possibility of knowing and experiencing God. To know something means to assimilate it intellectually and to adapt our own approach to the object. The instrument of knowledge must be as superior as possible to the object of knowledge. That is why physics and chemistry are more exact sciences than zoology or even psychology. For the closer we come to complex structures, the more difficult it becomes to know them. When our intellect is applied to superior objects, we should expect *a priori* that the results would be intellectually less satisfactory than in other instances. It is as though a two-dimensional being were reflecting on the existence of three-dimensional beings. It would certainly not be able to arrive at an adequate knowledge of them. But it would have some intimation, and it would formulate some poetic statements which, seen from a superior position, might sound quite remarkable. This might be man's situation in seeking to know God.

To sum up: religious intimation transcends religious experience and is expressed in religious poetry. Religious experience is open to further intimations, which reach forward into a dark room that is very difficult to illuminate. Religious symbols which shine into this room cannot be completely justified either by experience or by argument; but it can be shown that in view of the particular structure of the object, any basis in argument must inevitably be rejected. For wherever man not only investigates partial aspects of reality but seeks to order and clarify his relationship to reality as a whole, he goes beyond the already established conditions of his knowledge and experience.

One point to conclude with: the boundary between religious experience and intimation can be shifted. Some people have religious experiences in a sphere which for us is a matter for religious intimation. It might well be sensible to listen to them and not reject their experiences simply because they are not our own. Such people adopt the role of revealers towards their fellow-men.

2. Are religious commandments suggestions?

Religion consists in more than a perception of resonance and absurdity and sensitivity towards them. In religion, rather, experiences of resonance and absurdity come to have important effects on motivation: the holy is experienced as an appeal, as an 'ought', an imperative, at least where that conversion takes place in which the holy becomes a motive force and man becomes a response, knowing himself to be 'asked', 'involved' and 'put under obligation'. Any man with even a small degree of religious sensitivity will have such an experience. And the words used to describe it will always be similar. It is as though someone spoke to us, as though someone said, 'You must change your life'. Resonance and absurdity become an imperative experience. We seem to be encountered by a personal demand. It is here that we find the roots of the sociomorphic and psychomorphic interpretation of the holy: man seems to be a partner and a fellow-worker with personal deities. From them he receives commands, instructions for conduct and impulses for action. If this experience of an imperative were only an illusion, then religion, too, would contain no truth. If religion governed only our emotional attitude, and not our action and our ethics, it would not be important. But at this very point the modern criticism of religion announces its doubts. In the well-justified view of many philosophers, imperatives can never be derived logically from indicatives. There is a gulf between 'is' and 'ought'. So what would be the use of being able to justify the indicative aspects of religious experience in the face of the suspicion that they are merely projections, if this did not result in any call to action? What would be the use of demonstrating structural affinities between man and his environment, which can be experienced in religion, if their imperative force were mere suggestion? Such a suggestion might seem similar to that conveyed by a familiar study. It seems to say, 'You ought to work.' Yet the connection between room and work is only a matter of habit, which lends the room imperative force. Thus the suspicion that the imperative is a matter of suggestion is in fact the suspicion that those who derive imperatives from structures of being have earlier projected an imperative on to the structures of being.

Applied to religion, this means that in each case the different religions have projected their values and norms on to the universe, so as to be able to derive them from it again. For example, the warlike properties of a tribe were explained in terms of a god of war; in turn, belief in a warlike god served to justify the aggressive attitude of a tribe. Or another example: our valuation of love is read into reality so that we can say that God is love. In turn, the commandment to love is then derived from this understanding of God. These critical arguments, too, are difficult to reject. Rather, we must try to think them through to the end. So we shall adopt their standpoint and first of all assume that we ourselves must be responsible for our norms and imperatives, and that it is impossible to derive these norms and imperatives from pre-existing structures. In such conditions, can there be religious experience with the character of appeal? Can it have the power of conviction?

(a) Religious experience as a motivating force for ethical conduct
Philosophical criticism insisted emphatically on the separation of 'is' and 'ought', but it also made attempts to bridge this gulf; while

value judgments cannot be derived from judgments on facts, they can be corrected by them. For example, 'ought' always also implies 'can'. It is ridiculous to formulate an imperative which is quite incapable of being realized. Now whether it can be realized can only be established on the basis of facts. For example, should it be impossible for a teacher always to be able to be responsible for every pupil, it would be nonsense to put forward such a requirement. Thus while no positive imperatives can follow from facts, at least negatively they have a certain normative force: facts can help us to understand what we should not attempt. There are other such bridges between 'is' and 'ought': we can test norms to see if they are free from contradiction, for their relationship to existing norms, and for concealed interests. We can illuminate their historical derivation. We can investigate the conditions in which they might be realized, and analyse side effects. All this is still a matter of judging facts. So even a science strictly limited to the investigation of facts can build certain bridges between 'is' and 'ought'. Should not religion be even more capable of that? Certainly its bridging principles are not theoretical. They provide motivation. For in religious experience the reality around us becomes a motivating force. Granted, religion cannot relieve us of responsibility for our evaluations and decisions, but it can give us courage to act once we have seen what is the right thing to do. It can sustain us when we are caught up in the consequences of our mistakes. The strength of its motive force lies in the way in which it understands our evaluation, action and decision as a response to the fields of resonance and absurdity in reality. Even if in the last resort we have to discover the answer for ourselves, it is called forth by the appeal of the reality that surrounds us.

Reality experienced in a religious way motivates us in accordance with the principles which motivate human behaviour in other respects.[20] If we ask ourselves what sets human action going ('motivate' means 'move'), we can choose three starting points.

Most important are the stimuli inherent in a particular situation. It is easier to take action when we have positive experience of the external situation which prompts an invitation. For instance, it is easier to work in a familiar room than in a strange room. Granted, these are only external stimuli. Much more important are the internal stimuli implied by the situation: the tensions and contradictions which arouse in us the effort to seek some resolution of them. For example, the motivation for this book lies in the tension between critical awareness and traditional religion. The effort to balance out these tensions is a powerful spur towards reflection.

A second starting point for motivation leading to action can be found in the results of action. Here it may be a matter of purely external consequences. As he is writing, an author may look forward to the time when his book will be published and read. The 'intrinsic' results of the action are incomparably more important. Anticipation of the end of a book is a stimulus quite independent of the consequences that a manuscript may have. The theoretical mastery of a problem has a value in itself.

After the stimuli to action and the results of a work, a further important motive force is its direction. One can either take bearings from successful models or feel a need to pursue an independent course. Thus when writing, an author usually has some models in mind which gave him courage to express his thoughts consistently. At the same time, however, he is stimulated by his awareness that he is shaping his work himself, going new ways and acting without models.

All the starting points for motivating stimuli presuppose that the person to be motivated already has provisionally determined expectations, motives and concerns. There have to be quite definite aesthetic expectations before a room appears beautiful. It is the need for totality and balance that allows tensions to be experienced as stimuli, and so on. Psychologists describe this situation by saying that motivation presupposes motive. Interpreters would say that circumstances never provide motivation in themselves, but only in so far as they are perceived in the light of a certain pre-understanding.

The more experiences of resonance a man has, the more positive is his experience of reality. Now if – according to the assumptions of the theory of motivation – action is the more probable when the setting is a positive one, this experience of resonance may be said to be a force which encourages activity. It increases our delight in action, our courage to live. To use a simile: the religious man enters reality as though he were going into an elegant room, with attractive pictures and stylish furniture. Here, he feels, he cannot act like a clown. The whole atmosphere of the room requires him to behave accordingly. He is irritated by other people who do not feel the attraction of the room. He is even more irritated by the discovery that it still has dark corners in it. He feels their absurdity deeply, and it can cramp his actions.

However, the very conflict between the experiences of resonance and absurdity can also have motivating force. Conflicts perceived by a man prompt in him a tendency to act so as to diminish these conflicts, to solve problems, to reduce tension. In view of the conflict between resonance and absurdity, light and darkness, salvation and lostness, he feels called on to expand the field of the possible experience of resonance, so that it also sheds light on areas which are now in the darkness of absurdity and meaninglessness. To go back to the simile: the religious man does not just experience reality as a well-furnished room. He discovers other rooms in the house, a cellar in darkness, in which men live on the scraps of food consumed above in the light. He discovers dungeons and torture chambers. And he experiences the contradiction between the good and the bad rooms as an invitation to bring light to the dark rooms. We must therefore extend our previous definition of religion: religion is not only sensitivity to resonance and absurdity, but identification with the field of resonance and resistance against its absurdity. It is an unconditional drive towards the realization of an increasingly comprehensive field of resonance in reality.

Reality beyond human relationships does not completely contradict our concern and our longing for happiness. Sometimes, amazingly, it comes to meet us. Sometimes it brings us success. It confirms us, if only fragmentarily, though without meaning to. Assuming that its character as invitation were pure suggestion, a reflection of our longing for resonance, this longing would still be changed by this reflection: it would be longing partially fulfilled, purpose confirmed, an imperative strengthened by the indicative. To give an example: if we resolve on a decision to act rationally which is hard to justify – i.e. to orient our behaviour on arguments, even where reason has only a feeble chance of asserting itself – it is an enormous encouragement that nature too has a rational structure. And while we may never be able to derive the imperative 'You must act rationally' from reality as a whole, we may still be certain that we are acting in accordance with reality. The experience of nomological resonance strengthens our individual rationality. Accordingly, while the imperative might have its origin in ourselves, its intensification by the indicative would be contingently grounded in the structure of the reality around us, which does not completely contradict our needs and purposes, but sometimes comes to meet them, with positive consequences.

However, religiously motivated action is not unconditionally concerned with contingent support derived from reality around us, with success and recognition. It can be an end in itself; it can be experienced as meaningful in itself, regardless of any consequences. In any case, all the consequences of our actions are like drops of rain disappearing into the sea. What we achieve is nothing in the light of eternity. But light can still shine from a useless and unsuccessful act: even the most insignificant act can acquire a value which points beyond it, if it is seen in a religious context: as an element of the field of resonance in reality and as a contradiction of absurdity and meaninglessness. For a religious man, such awareness of involvement in the field of resonance in reality can be so valuable that even a completely involuntary action can have the stamp of eternal meaning for him. To share in the field of resonance of reality is of value in itself.

Like all human action, that motivated by religion is oriented on models: on Moses, Buddha, Socrates, Jesus, Gandhi or Albert Schweitzer. The lives of such normative figures show how we can truly respond to the field of resonance in reality and combat its absurdity: laziness, stupidity, violence, suffering. They also make it possible for followers who may not be capable of a creative response to the invitation contained in reality to live a life modelled on them. Little by little they have shown us the field of resonance in reality.

The nature of the invitation presented by reality experienced in religious terms is not clear to us. It encounters us as an indefinite obligation to which we have to respond by taking a particular obligation upon ourselves, even if we begin by imitating existing models of responsive conduct. Since no one can start completely from scratch, all religions offer relief from a burden by presenting particular specific norms. In the last resort, however, we ourselves are responsible for our ethical norms. And awareness of this can itself provide a motivation: we are more involved when a demand is made of us, when something important depends on our direction, creativity and decision. Our ethical awareness becomes greater when we realize that we can examine and modify our norms, and that an appeal to tradition is not enough. Self-directed motivation is therefore the highest form of motivation, even in actions influenced by religion. It should not, however, be seen as an independent, arbitrary and free expression of human will, but as an answer to the indeterminate element of appeal in reality.

(b) Religious experience as the foundation of ethical norms
We have seen that religious experience is significant in motivating our ethical action. Ethical action presupposes a trust in reality. The

61

world must be constructed in such a way that, at the least, it is not nonsensical to act ethically in it. The field of resonance in reality must be stronger than all absurdity: or, to put it more cautiously, it must be of greater significance to the man acting ethically than an often overwhelming sense of absurdity. Now the ethical problem does not just consist in the question of the origin of our drive towards action. The ethical question is: how can I decide whether I should follow a particular drive or not? How can I distinguish between valuable and detrimental aims? Indeed, must I not always recognize particular norms and values, if I am to experience a situation as providing a motive? At any rate, this conclusion follows from our theoretical considerations about motivation: the experiences of resonance and absurdity can only present their appeal and their imperative if man has already contributed a longing for resonance and horror of absurdity. Only then are structural affinities between man and the reality that surrounds him experienced in a positive way; only then can they exercise the function of strengthening and confirming. To make a general statement: motivation always presupposes motives, expectations, values, norms, standards, in the light of which the situation is viewed. The discrepancy between motive and situation leads to action which seeks to overcome it, and the recollection of situations in which the motives found fulfilment lends confidence and courage to our activity. But motives are introduced into the situation by us. Must we then concede that the appellative and imperative element in religious experience is a projection of our own motives? Are subjective ethical norms not always already presupposed, when religious experience provides a motive?

In fact, we have already implied that particular structural affinities between man and his environing reality are a satisfying experience of resonance. In and around us, however, we also find a blind and destructive energy which is alien to us. The dark side in us also finds an affinity. Yet we do not include such experiences of affinity among our significant experiences of resonance. Anyone who finds that they give strength and provide a motive is (to put it in an old-fashioned way) of the devil. Now the problem becomes more acute. Instead of deriving ethical norms from religious experience we find that religious experience already presupposes particular norms. Is it pure arbitrariness if we feel experiences of resonance to be significant – i.e. view them in the light of positive norms? Are these chance, historically conditioned, transitory norms?

No – limitless ethical relativism is transcended when it is experienced as an oppressive problem. Just as radical epistemological doubt leads at least to the one certainty of the *cogito ergo sum,* so ethical despair at the relativity of all norms at least leads to one conviction. If we could forgo the search for ethical obligation and content ourselves with a private 'I am for or against', there would no longer be an ethical problem. It would only be a political one; who wins? Only when someone says 'I cannot be for something unless you are also for it', and then finds out that there is no reason which will convince another person that his own decision was necessary, is there cause for ethical despair. The concern of other people is thus the condition for the possibility of radical ethical despair. Ethical despair that no values may be binding presupposes that there is at least one binding value: the assent of other people. Any justification of my conduct presupposes that I take the other people to whom I justify myself as seriously as I take myself. Thus any ethical reflection is grounded in a fundamental experience of resonance: in resonance between human beings, in the experience that the other man is akin to me and that I must act so that he understands me just as if I were standing in his place and he in mine. Whereas particular ethical norms may not have religious foundations, the unconditional obligation to formulate ethical norms cannot be derived from ethical premises, but is grounded in the experience of religious resonance. It becomes deeper and more universal the more the whole of reality, and not just one's fellow-man, is seen as partner. At this moment, in fact, ethics becomes the response to the whole complex of reality and we have to justify ourselves not only to the other man but to the field of resonance of all being.

But does this solve the problem? Ethical awareness presupposes resonance between partners. Experiences of resonance in turn presuppose a longing for resonance, i.e. a subjective response. However, is it not the case that it is we who bring a light into the world, by which it can be experienced as beneficial and meaningful? Now our subjective longing for resonance is not only strengthened by the reality around us; often enough that reality actually arouses it, calls it forth and shapes it. By virtue of his relatively unspecialized structure of drives, man does not just have specific concerns. Over and above all his basic physical needs he has an abundance of unspecified needs which do not allow him to live by bread alone. These unspecific needs are first given direction, definition and form through encounter with the surrounding reality: that is, man does not approach reality with a specific longing for resonance. He does not know what to look for in it. The longing for resonance in its manifold forms only comes alive in him through long and wearisome processes of adaptation to the objective structures of reality. Only gradually does he develop the motives in the light of which reality makes its appeal to him. There was a long period before he looked for nomological resonance in nature. And there was a long period before he ceased to regard mastery as the normal relationship between people and human groups, preferring a pattern of behaviour and mutual understanding in which mastery is reduced to the bare essentials. The longing for resonance was formed and developed only through a long struggle with the environment. We might say that objective reality itself evoked it. Our subjective motives are in the last resort the product of objective factors, an echo of total reality, just as the longing for love is an echo of love experienced, and remembrances seen in a positive light (i.e. something indicative) are effective as motives in new situations (which thus lends them the character of an appeal). Now if religious motives are in the last resort an echo of objective reality, it follows that there are no *a priori* religious motives; they can only be handed down and learned. The only *a priori* is the possibility of having a religious experience of reality. However, when this comes about, it is always historically conditioned. The imperative elements of religious experience therefore have different forms in the different religions. But it is always the case that the imperative experienced through religion corresponds to a human structure of need that has come about historically. Just as there is a specific structural need behind the appeals from reality sensed in the animal world, which has adapted itself to its environment by long processes, so man is influenced by a structure of needs which has become historical, so that he experiences the fields of resonance and absurdity in reality as an overwhelming appeal, concerned less with the pre-programmed needs of life and survival than with the changing needs of our spiritual life which are closely connected with them. Man is directed towards a home in which all things are familiar and men are found together as brothers; he longs for a world which he can affirm, because he feels himself affirmed by it. It is the need for the courage to live, to find a basis in reality and to be able to resist all experiences of absurdity. This courage to live is endorsed, furthered, strengthened by any experience of resonance, but is shattered, put to the test, questioned, by the experience of absurdity. Often, of course, it is deepened and continued, but often it is also destroyed. This yes to life is directed to the experience of resonance and therefore encounters us almost automatically as an appeal to seek, to make possible and to hope for further experience of resonance, and not to be overcome by the all-pervasive absurdity of life – by that sense of disorder which, to put it in theriomorphic terms, 'prowls around like a roaring lion, seeking someone to devour' (I Peter 5.8).

Thus the central religious imperative is: make possible the experience of resonance! Resist absurdity! But it is indefinite. Each religion and each society has a different way of making it specific, each has different experiences of resonance and absurdity at the heart of its interpretation of the world. Furthermore, in the last resort, we cannot explain why we accord decisive significance to the field of resonance in reality. Why not to experiences of absurdity? Why should we further and heighten life instead of continuing the alienation of life from itself: devouring and being devoured? Why should we practise love instead of following the laws of the jungle? Why should not the social Darwinism which is so widely practised be an appropriate response to reality? It is hard to give any logical reason why the field of resonance in reality should be exalted to become the decisive authority in our life. For the religious man, of course, that is self-evident. Once he has made the basic religious decision for the field of resonance in reality, or more exactly, once he has been driven to such a decision, then certain general tendencies in behaviour become an unconditional obligation for him and he can follow the great religious traditions in formulating these guidelines for action:

Affirm existence without prior conditions, even if you cannot give reasons! Investigate and observe the laws, rules and affinities within reality!

Preserve and enhance life around you; reduce grief and anxiety, hunger and sickness!

Further everything that makes possible love and understanding among men!

Take up the cause of all people and groups who are humiliated, despised and imposed upon!

Look for and create beauty!

Such concerns are general. Precisely what we should do is left to our imagination and our creativity. But all 'commandments' can be understood as an expression of love, a love which points beyond

65

the human sphere, a deep feeling of belonging together with all things and all creatures which finds its consummation in love between human beings: 'God is love, and he who abides in love abides in God and God in him' (I John 4.16).

We have explored the possibility that religion is a matter of suggestion. It is now time to sum up. Our starting point was the hypothesis that the imperative element contained in religious experience is a projection of our needs on to the reality around us; between the indicative of the world we experience and the imperative of ethical action there is a gulf which seems only to be bridged by a self-deception which takes place in religious experience. We saw that the gulf between 'is' and 'ought', indicative and imperative, is not absolute. Religious experience in the indicative motivates ethical behaviour, by strengthening our confidence in reality and making the discrepancy between resonance and absurdity a spur to our action. It is true that there are problems in deriving an imperative from an indicative, but an imperative can be derived from two indicatives: from a past experience and a contradictory present situation which is experienced negatively in the light of the past experience. The contradiction between two indicatives leads to the imperative if one accepts the premise that contradictions must be removed. Thus while it is true to say that religious experience only acquires motivating force when it is set in the light of subjective concerns (i.e. in the light of particular norms and expectations which we introduce into a situation), these subjective norms and expectations are the aftermath of past experiences. It is only because we have had indicative experiences of resonance that in new situations we experience an imperative discrepancy between our expectations of resonance and the given situation. Indeed, all motives and norms are the results of a long historical struggle with reality, and they need to be strengthened constantly through the reality around us. Thus all motives and norms are historical. We have to respond to them. But for that very reason they are part of a responsive attitude to the whole of reality; they are a response to the invitation presented by the field of resonance and absurdity around us, an answer to the appeal that goes out from our fellow man. The need to formulate ethical norms and to justify our own behaviour presupposes the religious experience of a deep-rooted affinity between all men, so that someone else can put himself in my place and vice versa. Without this religious experience, any ethic is built on sand.

(c) Religious experience and the crises of ethical action

Religion is indeed the basis of ethics, but it is more than ethics. For many, it only begins where ethical action is in crisis. We can distinguish three crises in ethical action.

First, ethical action is undeniably involved in a crisis of motivation when the world proves to be ethically irrational, i.e. when it becomes doubtful whether there is any 'advantage' at all in acting ethically; where the crafty or unscrupulous action is often more successful than the result of ethical sensitivity. Minor experiences of injustice are enough to give the impression that the world is ethically absurd and that ethical concern in it is meaningless. The question becomes even more pressing in the case of the immeasurable suffering of the innocent. The problem is: how can confidence in reality be maintained even in the face of its apparent ethical absurdity? Why act ethically if reality as directly experienced penalizes such action rather than confirming it? Beyond question, this is a fundamental problem of human existence, to which all religions seek to give an answer: even if they are thought to be inadequate, new attempts at an answer will always have religious features.

The second crisis of ethical action arises from man's experience of himself. He experiences not only the objective absurdity of the world but also his own guilt, failure, misconduct. He experiences his own subjective absurdity. The religious man who is gripped by the field of resonance in reality feels more strongly than others his inability to respond to it. He feels his deep alienation from it, his stupidity, his laziness, his introversion; with horror he perceives in himself a proneness to degeneracy, which goes against all his convictions and yet is very much part of him. He sees how against his will, he provokes conflict and aggression, instead of furthering love and understanding. And even if he pursues noble aims, he is caught up in wrong-doing while attempting to realize them. He feels what the religious tradition calls 'sin', subjective absurdity. Beyond question, every religion must be judged by the way in which it copes with this crisis of ethical action and helps us to overcome subjective absurdity.

In the two crises outlined above, the validity of ethical norms remained unshaken. On the contrary, the world and man's life were measured by them and the feeling of absurdity became greater because man's experience of himself and the world went against recognized ethical norms. The ethical crisis of the modern world has

67

gone one stage further. It is now questioned whether there are any binding norms at all by which human conduct can be measured. Today people are probably guided by a moderate sociological relativism; the norms are whatever is accepted as a norm in a given society, which is not a very satisfactory answer. Some people feel justified in questioning all the norms in a society as well as the form of that particular society, though in any society there are norms which may be more binding than their social framework. But sociological relativism is unsatisfactory. Man's ethical awareness will always consist in a search for norms and standards that go beyond the bounds of society and cultures. In our time religion is to be judged by the degree to which it takes account of this longing for binding values, and above all by the degree to which it is the foundation of all obligations: it has to present as a central experience the deep bonds which exist between all men, regardless of their ethnic origins, culture, status and age.

We can only raise the questions here. But no religion today can remain alive without giving an answer to them, and unless they are answered there can be no motive for ethical action. The Christian is convinced that in his encounter with the figure of Christ he finds an answer to the crisis of ethical consciousness; that his eyes are open once and for all to the bond that exists between all men; and his belief provides an unconditional motivation which is stronger than all objective and subjective absurdity. However, that is to anticipate the final chapter. For Christian faith is *one* answer to religious problems. First we must ask, in quite general terms, how religious symbols are connected with ethical action.

(d) Religious symbols and ethical conduct

Traditional religion has always combined ethical commands and religious symbols: remember the impact of that majestic voice from Sinai! Or the impressive story about the night in which the Koran was received! Why do we keep coming up against a connection between religious poetry and ethical commands? Why does myth lie at the foundation of norms?

We saw how religious symbols go beyond the sphere of religious experience. They extend into that dark area of religious intimations of whose existence we may be convinced, even if it is inaccessible to us. However, there are also practical reasons for the intensification, over-extension and transformation of religious experience in symbols and myths. When it comes to motivation reality is open-ended. It does not tell us what to do. It is not

68

unequivocal. We have to specify and interpret its indeterminate claim by means of a long struggle. All religions have done this by interpreting open-ended structures of reality in terms of symbols and myths which provide clear and unequivocal motivation. In this way they change reality through a symbolic transformation of experience: through actions with more or less complex signs; through narrative, speculation and fantasy. Day by day we are concerned with the symbolic transformation of reality. Our preoccupation continues even at night, as our dreams indicate. We must adapt reality to ourselves by symbolic actions in order to make it our home. Myth and cult are symbolic actions of this kind, in which we identify ourselves with the field of resonance in reality and resist absurdity, in order to make a home for ourselves.

The important thing here is that the symbolic actions of myth go back to objective factors. They give shape to the experience of the holy which is grounded in the objective structures of reality. However, the transformation of them into symbols goes back to creative acts of human imagination. Imagination here is not meant to be a derogatory term. On the contrary: in the creative acts of his mythical imagination, man expresses both his sense of an inaccessible mystery in the depth of all reality and his own attitudes, decisions and values: the life he lives and the life he does not live; his conscious and his unconscious motives; his manifest properties and those which he has not yet realized. To illustrate the connection between reality and imagination we might adduce the projective tests which are used in psychological diagnosis: they present shapes with very little structure and a good deal of ambiguity. The person being tested has to interpret these shapes and give them structure; for instance, he may see two striking ink blots as the wings of a butterfly or a bat or as something else – though none of these interpretations is entirely apt. The evaluation of such tests begins from the fact that those asked to provide an interpretation project themselves on to the relatively open material, so that what they sense of what is presented to them gives some indication of their motives and attitudes. The same thing happens in religion: man is confronted with the fields of resonance and absurdity. His interpretations relate to something that is objectively to hand. They are not arbitrary. He senses something behind the structures that present themselves to him. But once he talks about what he senses, he has to read his own understanding of himself, his attitudes, his values and concerns into the reality that he is to interpret.

69

Thus, for example, in myth the manifold appeals to man from the environment are intensified in such a way that they become the activities of deities. The conflict between resonance and absurdity becomes the fight between God and Satan, between the Son of God and the devils, between the powers of light and the powers of darkness. And there is probably no more gripping chapter in our history than the history of religion, in which man uses imagery from his imagination to fight against the absurdity that threatens him, seeks to destroy Satan and longs for his lost home, so that in the end the tears will be wiped away from all eyes. However, divine action is really always symbolic human action as well. When the Athenians told how Athene chose their city to dwell in, they enacted symbolically in the myth their identification with their home. It was the same when the Jewish people spoke of their election by Yahweh and of his promise of a land flowing with milk and honey.

Once we become aware that symbolic actions are projections we can no longer accept them as the expression of a reality which is affirmed by dogma. They become sacred poetry. We can accept this poetry, because it is based on the indisputable religious experience of resonance and absurdity in reality. But we must remember that it goes beyond this experience in giving us some intimation of the mystery of reality which transcends all concepts, reading our motivations and attitudes into its obscurity.

Anyone who requires that we should believe in this sacred poetry, in the sense of holding it to be true, does harm to religion, for all his good intentions; he makes it incredible. Those who seek to impose such belief on the members of a community by administrative measures corrupt religious life; for in so doing they only create dishonesty, hypocrisy and forbidden areas of thought. They prevent the possibility of open communication about the basic questions of life. We must reach the point when we can say openly that a large part of our religious tradition is fiction and poetry.

It is easier to make this concession if we are aware that truth is hidden in, with, and under religious projections. That must be our final judgment on the question. Such truth is not just poetic truth; religious experience is founded in an objective reality. Religion consists in the attempt to live life as a response to the whole of reality. Cognitively, it discloses structural affinities between our existence and the reality around us. Emotionally, it makes us sensitive to the abundance of resonance in reality and also offers security in the face of the threat from the absurd. And in terms of motive it gives us courage to live, motivation to do what we have recognized to be right in response to the field of resonance in reality, although we are continually caught up in wrong actions. All religious traditions are to be measured by the degree to which they fulfil these functions. The standard by which we measure them is a specifically religious one. This is the only way in which enlightenment can take place in the context of religion, rather than religion taking place in the context of the enlightenment, a process which so far has always led in the end to enlightenment without religion.

IV · The Problem of Historical Relativity

So far we have treated the problem of religion in very general terms. But religion exists only in the form of particular religions. This gives rise to our third main problem. Can critical faith build on one particular religious tradition? Are there sufficient grounds for preferring one particular tradition to others? And if one particular tradition is preferred, can it then have an unconditional character? Does it not lose its absolute validity simply by virtue of the fact that we are aware how much our religious convictions depend on the chances of place, time, descent and personal career? Especially in Germany, we are aware that had we been born only a few miles away, we would have had a different family background, have grown up in very different surroundings. We might perhaps have become enthusiastic about things over which we are now mildly sceptical. We might perhaps have come to despise what means most to us. We fool ourselves if we claim that we become Christians, Marxists, or whatever, solely on the basis of critical reflection. True, critical reflection can help us to detach ourselves from a tradition in which we have naively grown up, but in that case we remain tied to it in a negative way; we remain erstwhile Protestants or converted Marxists without anyone being able to challenge the reality of our conversion. The problem is: can we identify ourselves with the Christian tradition and at the same time do justice to the claims of critical rationality, if that tradition is conditioned by historical relativity? For one thing is certain: it is no argument simply to say that one has grown up in Christianity.

If we reject the glorification of blind decisions made by groups which pride themselves on irrationality, and the rationalist illusion that one reaches conclusions in religious questions only by proven arguments, we are left with four possible approaches which may help us to clarify our decision: arguments from the nature of tradition and historical influence; theoretical and anthropological arguments. The argument from the nature of tradition can reassure us that we are following a tradition and in so doing are taking over

72

elements which are inevitably unproven. Of course this argument is valid for all traditions. The argument from historical influence can explain why we should be intensively concerned with the Christian tradition, though that does not mean that we should identify ourselves with it. Arguments from the theory of religion can give plausible reasons why we should identify ourselves with the content of the Christian tradition, because it expresses religious truth. Finally, anthropological considerations can help us to understand why the Christian truth is bound up with a form of communication (the church's proclamation) which undergoes constant social renewal and can gain unconditional significance for individuals. All these considerations and arguments cannot relieve us of the need to make a decision. Identification with the Christian tradition always contains an element of decision; but this is not a blind decision, still less an adventure in metaphysics, which enjoys the uncertainty of one's own position as a stimulus bringing an added thrill in the way that a reckless climber enjoys the attraction of dangerous ascents and descents.

1. The nature of tradition

The argument from the nature of tradition is that critical rationality has an interest in utterly exhausting all traditions before abandoning them. To leave experiences and insights of past generations unused, to forget them or to repress them, goes against that nature. Indeed, it would be sheer delusion were anyone to suppose that they could simply begin all over again from the beginning. Without traditions we would all be religious illiterates (and illiterates in other respects as well). It can even make sense to have a dogmatic identification with a particular tradition: this prevents over-hasty death certificates on traditions as long as life remains in them. In essence, of course, the argument from the economy of tradition is anti-dogmatic: it is to the advantage of all traditions, philosophical and religious, Hindu and Christian, Catholic and Orthodox. Critical rationality cannot simply have an interest in the evaluation of one single tradition. It cannot devalue or reject other traditions without thorough examination. Furthermore, it can never reject the possibility that others may have had a better grasp of the truth. It must be open. Only this open dialogue between the traditions can match the religious longing for universal interpretative resonance. The time is long past when claims could be made that particular objective traditions were absolutes. Our ethical, religious and historical consciousness goes against such claims to absoluteness. Today the only possibility is that of an identification with our religious traditions backed up by tolerance.

2. The argument from historical influence

The justification for our primary concern with the Christian tradition lies in the influence which the biblical tradition has had. Here we can distinguish between its global and its European influence. Looking at mankind as a whole, we may claim that the European societies influenced by the Christian tradition were the first to create a system of communication between all peoples, cultures and traditions. The biblical tradition was not the only one to produce this result, nor was its effect simply positive: its negative contribution is horrifying. Nevertheless, Max Weber's question is still justified. Why did modern developments begin in Europe rather than anywhere else? Why was Europe the place from which a system of global communication was built up – despite the high level of culture among the Arabs, the Indians and the Chinese? Thus there is reason to be preoccupied with Christianity, simply because of the influence it has had. However, this argument should not be over-estimated. We should not forget that the Europeans have controlled and shaped the world for only about four hundred years – by virtue of military superiority, which has never been a good argument in spiritual matters. In the Middle Ages the Islamic and Chinese cultures were still superior to ours, or at least at the same level. And even today we have no reasons for self-satisfied Eurocentrism. We learn from the East, as the revival of meditative practices shows. And if there are many obscure phenomena, that only points to a deficiency among us, a starting-point for charlatans and obscurantists.

That apart, although we live in a culture influenced by Christianity, it is influenced by other factors than Christian tradition. Not everything that is dear and precious to us, not even everything that may prove valuable for a critical faith, can be derived from biblical tradition (though it may be reconciled with that tradition). Scientific curiosity, tolerance and humour; this-worldliness and sexual love and the awareness of beauty: all this is much closer to Greek than to biblical tradition. We should never forget that Christianity only exercised its influence in conjunction and in conflict with the traditions of Graeco-Roman antiquity. Theologians often underestimate this fact. Understandably they

74

tend to derive all that they prize in the present from biblical sources (and play down the significance of other ancient traditions). This is a very one-sided historical view, and often it is not very wise. Valuations of the present change quickly. Yesterday secularization was resisted as apostasy from Christianity; today it is celebrated as a legacy of it. Today theologians still lay stress on the connection between belief in creation and scientific control of nature; tomorrow they may well be praising the scepticism of the church about science and progress because the increase in environmental problems has brought such scepticism into fashion again (as though one could remove the shadow side of scientific and technological progress by subsequent glorification of tabus in religious thought). It is suspicious that in these and other reflections on the historical influence of religion the Greek traditions are not only denied but even devalued. One favourite argument is to divert criticism of Christianity so that it becomes criticism of the Greek traditions in Christianity, whether this is seen as a dualistic understanding of the world, hostility to corporeality or scurrilous speculation. What unfairness! Every historian knows how much Christianity is indebted to Greek traditions. Without them, it might even have atrophied into superstition. At least the Coptic church shows how Christianity could have developed in a different way from that demanded by philosophical thinking. So if we are going to adopt the argument from historical influence, i.e. that it is legitimate to be concerned with the particular traditions that determine one's environment, we do not have any justification for being concerned with Christianity only. There is an argument for being concerned with Christianity as it struggles with the traditions of ancient rationalism. Those who are aware of the historical influence of Christianity cannot dismiss philosophical and religious criticism as irrelevant to Christianity. Rather, the programme of an enlightenment in the context of religion will seem the consistent continuation of an argument which has gone on for centuries, and which develops independently of individual opinions and concerns: the controversy between the tradition of critical philosophical thought and religious faith. The idea of a critical faith which affirms its awareness of ideological, empirical and historical criticism of religion is equally at home in Jerusalem and in Athens; for the notion of a critical examination of what others believe goes back to Socrates.

Both Greek and Christian traditions come to us from a past which historically speaking is separated from us by at least two decisive turning points: the rise of modern science and modern social policies. The disciplined and methodical approach of the natural sciences has disclosed a field of nomological resonance the extent of which no one would ever have guessed at. The fact that the professional representatives of traditional religion have proved to be more irritated than pleased at this new dimension of religious belief should not prevent us from seeing the process as an extension and transformation of our religious experience. Presumably we have still to relate the results of the scientific investigation of the world and the significance of the discovery of an overwhelming regularity in the universe to our emotions and our motives. At all events critical faith requires a constant extension of the investigation of reality. Above all, it is a support for scientific curiosity. It does not discourage such curiosity, put pressure on it or regard it with mixed feelings.

The second decisive turning point in the history of religion came about with the rise of modern social policies: since then, the experience of resonance in human solidarity has been related to a changing and changeable society, for which man has to take on responsibility. Solidarity has become the central theme of religion – one might think of the definition of God as co-humanity, one-sided though that may be. In this process, of course, primal biblical ideas arise again. Yet here too traditional religions have had to undergo a difficult process of learning which others have faced before them: they have been confronted with a vehement ideological criticism for which nothing has seemed to be sacred, whether faith, tradition, or institution, because all have been too deeply entangled in notorious injustice. So traditional religions have fought such criticism off. But they have failed to recognize that in the last resort radical ideological criticism has been governed by an ethical and religious interest, namely unconditional concern for the lessening of suffering: social institutions and forms of legitimation are not criticized for their cynical delight in exposure, but because they have caused suffering. This is why ideological criticism has taken over the task of the prophets in their attacks on church and society.

A fleeting glance at the more recent history of religion shows that the forms of the holy are constantly given new definitions. Religious truth, too, is evolutionary. It is not given once and for all in particular traditions. Rather, these traditions undergo decisive changes in the process of exercising influence; modern men cannot view them in the same way as people from past times. Their influence has not been uninterrupted. In fact it could be said that the gaps which have been indicated in the history of the influence of ancient and biblical traditions are themselves a part of this history of their influence. They have been made possible only in the context of these traditions. Such a comment is true. However, it does not follow automatically that the traditions have a permanent validity. There is a functional autonomy[21] in historical phenomena; i.e., developments which led to the rise of the modern world need not be identical with developments which guarantee its survival. Historical phenomena can become independent of their origin. Therefore claims to legitimation and establishment cannot be derived from a history of particular influences. Some arguments must be rejected as false, e.g. that all Europeans have been influenced by Christianity; there is no good reason for the view that Christians are distinct only in that they regard as a matter of (subjective) conviction what for others is an unconscious (objective) matter of fact. The origin of the modern world and the foundations on which it is based are two different things. Conclusions cannot be drawn from the Christian past of our cultures to the hidden Christianity of our present – even if the changes from the past to the present were directed by Christian considerations.

There is no privileged access to traditions any more than there is a privileged access to knowledge. No assessment of the influence of biblical tradition in our time is credible if it does not take into account the importance of other traditions from antiquity, the breaks in tradition in the modern period and the functional autonomy of what has emerged from all this. Thus the history of the influence of biblical tradition can be the occasion for intensive preoccupation with it; but it can never be an intrinsic reason for identifying oneself with this tradition – Judaism and Islam have also been influenced historically by biblical traditions. We must therefore look for further reasons why we should identify ourselves with the Christian tradition.

3. Considerations based on the theory of religion

The only reason for identifying oneself with a particular religious tradition is the conviction that it does in fact present an appropriate solution to religious problems. Arguments based on the theory of religion must take the place of those based on its influence. We shall therefore consider two questions about religious traditions and their symbolism, namely: Which religious symbolism makes us most sensitive to experiences of resonance and absurdity? Which religious symbolism makes possible unconditional identification with the field of resonance in reality – against all absurdity? I shall claim that a struggle with experiences of resonance and absurdity is to be seen most clearly, most simply and most decisively in Christian symbolism. This is not a dogmatic evaluation of Christian symbols. They have a functional significance. If it could be shown that other symbols and statements accord better with the fundamental problems of religion, we would have to revise our attitude.

Thus the Christian tradition has to prove itself within the framework of a general theory of religion. But do the ideas expressed here really amount to a general theory of religion? Do they begin by putting the religious question in such a way that Christianity must prove to be the best answer? This question is justified. For the arguments and ideas presented here are influenced by Christianity, and their content is rooted in it. Thus the concept of resonance is governed by the Christian idea of love; the significance of the historical responsibility of men is an element in all biblical religions. Even our 'general' theory of religion is historically relative; it is part of the interpretation of biblical traditions. Does that mean that it is crypto-Christian dogmatics?

No one can escape historical conditioning. But we cannot rule out the possibility that generally valid insights can be attained from a historically conditioned perspective. Conclusions about the validity or invalidity of a set of ideas cannot be drawn from the particular context in which they arise. To put it in more specific terms: I am convinced that Christianity offers a contribution to religious problems which will stand up in open dialogue with other religions. Open dialogue is not only impeded by dogmatic claims to absoluteness: it is also impossible if one party involved has nothing to say. To concede, then, that the theory of religion put forward here is historically conditioned is not to pass judgment on its validity. We may legitimately read the Christian tradition as an answer to the basic question of religion, even if this basic question of religion may have been put in a way possible only within the confines of Christian tradition.

Christology stands at the centre of Christian tradition. Everything else is a prelude and an epilogue, footnotes and glosses. Consequently we may limit ourselves to christology, difficult though it may be to leave the Old Testament completely out of account. Our question is: Do the images and symbols of New

Testament christology give an appropriate answer to the fundamental problems of religion, i.e. to the conflict between experiences of resonance and experiences of absurdity?

(a) Five problems in dealing with the historical Jesus

Before we answer this question, we must sketch out five problems
which any discussion of Jesus poses to a faith which is shaped by
historical consciousness. These problems have oppressed theology
for more than two hundred years, but they have also led to fruitful
new developments. They appear in a new light when we read the
texts of the New Testament primarily in order to discover an
answer to the basic problems of religion, rather than looking for
historical guarantees for the church's dogma.

First, we have the problem of historical scepticism. Historical
research and, indeed, research of any kind, can only come to
hypothetical conclusions. Its results are valid only until they are
refuted. By contrast, faith looks for certainty. It also looks for
certainty about the historical Jesus, but here it is disappointed by
scientific criticism, because critics cannot say with any degree of
assurance which words and traditions of Jesus are historical and
which are not. All it has to offer is a collection of hypotheses, some
probable and some improbable, and none of them completely certain. Surely it would be stupid to base one's life on scientific
hypotheses which keep changing so quickly?

One thing, however, can be taken as certain, namely, the present
text of the New Testament, regardless of doubts as to what parts of
it are invention and what parts truth, what parts are original and
what parts are secondary. Here we find an impressive picture of
the figure of Jesus. Now at this point, religious interest is not
concerned with the complicated question of which elements in this
picture are historical and which are not. Only one question matters. What solution do these pictures of Jesus provide to the fundamental problem of religion? Religious truth is self-evident,
regardless of the question of historicity; it is as self-evident as the
parables in the Bible, which do not claim to be historical. However, once anyone becomes convinced that the New Testament
texts contain an abiding truth which is capable of changing men's
lives, he or she may become quite legitimately interested in the way
in which the pictures of Jesus arose, and in their connection with
the historical Jesus. First and foremost, however, comes an interest
in the actual truth-content of the New Testament. If we were to
assume that the disciples of Jesus had invented all these miraculous

79

statements and stories, would that be an argument against their intrinsic truth?

At all events, this much seems probable.[22] The picture of Jesus contained in the synoptic gospels was shaped by the Jesus movement in Syria and Palestine in the fifty years or so after Jesus' death. As far as we can judge, there was a relatively large degree of continuity between the thinking and life-style of Jesus and that of his disciples, so that the basic features of the traditional picture of Jesus may well go back to the historical Jesus. Differences from this picture of Jesus only began to arise when Christianity entered the Hellenistic world. Paul stresses the mythical Christ-event. John presents a kind of synthesis between the picture of the earthly Jesus and his transfiguration in the light of a mythical event between heaven and earth.

Next, there is the problem of historical relativity. Even if we had a picture of Jesus immune to the attacks of historical scepticism, we would still have to solve the problem of historical relativity in religions. For now it is becoming increasingly clear that Jesus and the christological poetry which he inspired can only be understood in the context of Near Eastern religion. For example, as Jesus' message of the imminence of the kingdom of God demonstrates, he stands in an apocalyptic tradition. Christological poetry cannot be understood apart from the intensive controversy with its environment in which primitive Christianity was involved. Of course, the way in which the New Testament is embedded in its environment brings out its originality and its uniqueness: a comparison with apocalyptic texts makes the distinctive character of the message of the kingdom of God even clearer. Without question, Jesus and faith in him represent a unique event, like all historical phenomena. But it would be wrong to suppose that the first Christians found only the unique elements of their faith important, as though even then they shared the modern passion for originality, which attaches value only to what is different, new and special. The way in which the New Testament is embedded in its environment presents no difficulties to anyone who approaches it primarily with a religious question: Why should the religious world of Jesus' time not have had important insights of its own? Why should we not welcome the fact that the content of the New Testament took up, illuminated and transformed the intimations and the longings of many men? Why should we not rejoice over the interpretative resonance that we can detect between the varied phenomena of the history of religion? Does a truth become valueless because it is

80

witnessed to by many people? The first apologists spoke of the *logos spermatikos* – a hidden meaning present everywhere – which could be found among all peoples. This was a good notion, which has wrongly been made tabu in modern Protestant theology.

Thirdly, we have the problem of historical remoteness or interpretation. Even if we had an absolutely reliable picture of the historical Jesus which proved different in every respect from other phenomena in the history of religion (a day-dream of many theologians), we would be left with the problem of the alien character of Jesus. His belief in demons, his expectation that the world would soon come to an end and his radical approach might seem not only alien, but repulsive, to many of our contemporaries. Granted, all these features can be explained against the background of their time. But this means taking Jesus back into the grey mists of a past world; there does not seem to be much of a message for the present. Thus we have the paradox that historical-critical research usually begins with a love of the traditions which it investigates, but leads to a feeling of growing alienation; and in the end, love of Jesus is accompanied by the fear that he may be taken away by force, by the attempt continually to use reinterpretation in order to keep him in line with contemporary trends. Does not a regard for Jesus require that we should leave him in his age? It is quite a shock to become properly aware of the problem for the first time.

On the other hand, even in primitive Christianity we keep finding new pictures of Jesus in which Jesus is reinterpreted for a different audience. Modern christologies continue this history of interpretation. In what they say they almost always go beyond what can be achieved solely by historical-critical interpretation, and they do so in order to give the figure of Jesus an abiding significance for the present. It has to be conceded that no picture of Jesus which has moved men's hearts at any time in the history of Christianity is beyond the attacks of historical criticism. Conversely, the subtle hypotheses of historical-critical research have seldom changed men's hearts.

It might be objected that everyone has projected values and attitudes back on to the historical Jesus, instead of presenting them on their own authority. But one could equally well say that each of them illuminated one aspect of the historical Jesus, and it is an indication of the greatness of Jesus that he has kept provoking new attempts at understanding and misunderstanding. The wealth of interpretations speaks for him rather than against him, and cannot

81

be restricted by historical-critical research. Historical-critical research is hardly in a position to canonize particular interpretations; it can, however, at least protect us from one-sided and erroneous approaches. It leaves room for manoeuvre, and what use is made of this room depends on the religious experiences of any particular time. Here, to my mind, is the heart of the problem of interpretation. The Bible comes alive where authentic religious experience coincides with texts which are themselves testimony to an authentic religious experience: the past strikes a spark off the present or the present off the past, and both are illuminated. The chief reason why religious texts from the past are so difficult to understand is that modern man has become uncertain of his own religious experience. He mistrusts it, and expects his encounter with the past to supply information which he will obtain only if he is truly concerned with religious questions and experiences. Interpreters who lived before the modern age could still project their own experiences naively and unself-consciously on to texts from the past, in turn deriving such experiences from the texts. Modern interpreters, on the other hand, investigate the texts by means of historical criticism and then find that such interpretation does not lead to religious experience. The consequence is often trouble for their religious life in the present. They become technicians of tradition. Only one conclusion can be drawn from the problem as we have described it: it is important to be aware of one's present religious experiences and to articulate the degree of independence which they have from the past; or, to put it in academic terms, it is important to work out a theory of religion so that it then becomes possible to enter into a dialogue with the past which is no longer expected to meet the impossible demand that the present should be legitimated by the past. Such a dialogue would be open to the past. And again and again we shall have the pleasant surprise of finding unexpected allies there, indeed a better way of expressing things, which can give a new stimulus to religious life in the present.

The pictures of Jesus which emerge from such an interlocking of past and present experience make it unnecessary for us to look exclusively for historical-critical legitimation (even if these pictures are meant to be beyond the reach of historical criticism). They are their own religious justification, just as the picture of a beloved is a justifiable one for the lover, however much it may go beyond what others see (and overlook) in the beloved.

Then there is the problem of the continuity between the historical Jesus and the kerygmatic Christ. As we have seen, the problem of the way in which Jesus is related to interpretations of him already begins in the New Testament. The picture of Christ in the Hellenistic churches differs from the picture of Jesus in the synoptic gospels (and therefore from the historical Jesus). New Testament christology is a combination of history and fiction, poetry and truth. Without doubt, however, the historical Jesus gave rise to it. Granted, this christology does not reproduce the historical Jesus; it presents him in heightened symbolic form: christology is poetry about Christ – the transformation of the historical Jesus into the kerygmatic Christ through the symbolic actions of primitive Christian groups in which the birth of Jesus became the manifestation of a deity, the cross became an expiatory death which redeemed the universe, and the Easter visions became the enthronement of the new ruler of the world. It is impossible to believe that this imagery represents objective events: the appearance of a deity, his return to heaven and his rule over the universe. None of this can ever be verified; it is impossible to have a meaningful discussion of the objectivity of such ideas, even if one suspects that they point to a mystery which transcends our conceptuality. All that we can do is to allow the imagery to have as profound an influence as possible, to let it exercise its transforming power and make it possible for us to identify with that field of resonance in reality which can stand up to the overwhelming power of absurdity. In this regard it needs no 'objective' truth. It has its own intrinsic truth, or to put it more exactly, it has its objective point of reference in the fields of resonance and absurdity to be found in reality. It discloses this field and reveals it to us.

In that case, can we dispense with any quest for the historical Jesus? No. It is inevitable that people should be interested in the historical origins of christological poetry. Granted, recourse to the historical Jesus does not in itself provide a foundation for christological poetry, but this poetry does have its roots in history. It was shaped by historical events which continue to have an effect through it. When we take anything seriously, we want to know how it came into being. That is our only way of understanding it. In addition to this interpretative interest, there is a practical point of view: truth becomes more concrete when it is rooted in history, when we can see that all christological symbols and images are grounded in the life of a man and are inconceivable apart from this life. In that case we are not just dealing with empty proclamations; we are not following mere ideas and notions and declarations of intent, but a specific human being, who began to put into effect the concerns of the christological poetry in which he is enshrined. To this degree the question of the historical Jesus affects our concerns considerably. In so far as religion and ethics, faith and motivation belong together, we have to be interested in the historical Jesus.

Christian faith is necessarily interested in the historical, but it is based on the heightened symbolic forms in which the historical element is preserved, intensified and transcended. Attempts to ground faith in mere history usually seem feeble. Scholars use every possible exegetical artifice in dealing with sayings of Jesus suspected of being genuine until they come up with the desired result. Laudable though the concern for historical honesty expressed here may be, it fails to recognize the power of the 'poetry of the holy'. Karl Barth's christology may be naive in terms of historical criticism, but it does far more justice to the New Testament. In fact it has only one drawback. It presents as church dogmatics what is really religious poetry, i.e. a complex of symbolic actions with which men respond to the field of resonance and absurdity in reality and come to grips with it.

Lastly, we have the problem of truth. At all events, one question is decisive. What is the truth communicated by encounter with the figure of Jesus: not historical truth, not scientific truth, but religious truth, which is objectively grounded in the field of resonance and absurdity in reality and can permeate the whole of life? Only when we have found and recognized this truth do the other problems arise. What goes back to the historical Jesus? In what way does he differ from all others in the history of religion? What is his significance for the present? What holds the various interpretations of Christ in the New Testament together, and connects them with the historical Jesus? Can this truth be detached from the proclamation of the church? Can it make absolute claims? One problem today is that the truth expressed in the Jesus traditions is too little understood, and secondary aspects are made into primary ones. Thus Jesus is presented as the mediator of an unconditional call for decision – but for what reality has this decision to be made? Or the characteristic feature of the message of Jesus is seen to be its character as event – but it is not at all clear what actually happened. Or the claim of Jesus is presented as a crisis of religions – but what was this claim? Truth is always concrete. It has a definite content. Even the truth of New Testament christology does not consist in formal claims, or in tautologies like 'the revealer reveals that he is the revealer!'

(b) The truth of New Testament christology

Why should we accept the christological symbolism to which the historical Jesus gave rise? An early answer was that it discloses the demands of the universe to us, the abundance of its resonance and its absurdity. Where there are so many competing appeals, it brings clarity, by putting a suffering human being at the centre of heaven and earth and subordinating all other powers to him: all powers in heaven, on earth and under the earth. There can be few finer pieces of religious poetry than the hymn in Colossians 1.15ff., in the symbolism of which a crucified man is exalted above all cosmic powers and appeals, not to abolish them, but to integrate them, reconcile them and embrace them. No matter what man can experience as sacred – the ordered structure of nature, the aesthetic beauty of the world, the organic character of life and the magic of love – beyond all question it is a man who is put in the centre of the world's abundance of resonance and absurdity. In his light everything takes on a new appearance. All resonance becomes incarnate in him. He becomes the final criterion for everything that moves us and concerns us, terrifies us and fascinates us. He becomes the key and the mediator of our religious experience of reality. He becomes the revealer.

What the hymn in Colossians expresses in terms of christological poetry can be found earlier in the figure of the historical Jesus. In a mysterious way he spoke of the 'Man' who would soon appear to judge the world. The figure of the 'Man' (or the 'Son of Man') has an unmistakable anthropological stamp. In Daniel 7 he is contrasted with the beasts who symbolize the various kingdoms; in Matthew 8.20 with the foxes and the birds. In Mark 2.27f. a parallel is drawn between 'Son of Man' and 'men'; and in Matthew 25.31ff. he is identified with them. In this last passage, the 'Man' says:

> I was hungry and you gave me food,
> I was thirsty and you gave me drink,
> I was a stranger and you welcomed me,
> I was naked and you clothed me,
> I was sick and you visited me,
> I was in prison and you came to me.

And then he adds: 'As you did it to one of the least of these my brethren, you did it to me' (Matt. 25.45). The revolutionary feature of christological symbolism was clearly recognized in the christology of the early church when it coined the formula: God became man so that he might make men God. For now in fact every man has an unconditional quality of appeal and an unconditional value.

Christological symbolism makes us sensitive to the fundamental ambivalence of the holy, to both the fascination and the terror which it evokes. There could hardly be a more convincing symbol of the absurdity of human existence than the cross. In many places the Roman authorities used the cross to break down resistance. Crosses got in the way of the desires of oppressed groups for freedom. The cross was a humiliating punishment for the lower classes, for slaves and rebels. The cross of the historical Jesus was only one among many. The penalty of the cross was imposed on a man who had already proved dangerous as a result of his teaching and its effects, a man who championed a non-violent solution to human conflict. Symbolism heightened its significance even more. An exemplary and innocent man died on the cross. That was absurd enough. Yet there was even more to it than that. God himself died on the cross. In symbolic actions the wealth of resonance in reality came face to face with annihilation. Even 'God' was exposed to the ultimate absurdity. Nothing was immune from it. There is no impregnable fortress into which we can retreat in the face of the negativity of human existence. Everything, no matter how precious, meaningful, valid, can be wiped out by the all-pervasive force of absurdity. Those who live under the sign of the cross are made sensitive once and for all to the absurdity of human existence. In other words, those who reproduce the crucifixion of the Son of God in symbolic actions are made vulnerable to their innermost depths. What causes them terror can no longer be suppressed, no matter what form it takes.

At the same time, christological symbolism articulates the most powerful feeling of resonance in human experience, the experience of love: 'Whoever confesses that Jesus is the Son of God, God abides in him, and he is God. So we know and believe the love God has for us. God is love, and he who abides in love abides in God, and God abides in him' (I John 4.15f.). No matter how we interpret the details of this statement, one thing is clear: through love, the wealth of resonance in reality is revealed to us, and this comes about through men's love of one another: 'No man has ever seen God; if we love one another, God abides in us and his love is perfected in us' (I John 4.12). Thus christological poetry is love poetry, and anyone who makes it into a dogma is in effect seeking to transform a declaration of love into a legal contract.

What christological poetry expresses in heightened form could be found earlier in the life of the historical Jesus. Jesus sums up all religious and ethical commandments in the command to love (Mark 12.28ff.), and in making reconciliation with one's brother the prerequisite for reconciliation with God (Matt. 5.23f.), he is demonstrating one thing quite clearly. Unless we have an experience of resonance between human beings, we shall be shut off from the field of resonance in the rest of reality. Jesus shows quite vividly what is required in relations between human beings: relief of physical suffering, the healing of illnesses and personality disorders, the abolition of hunger, the removal of anxiety, hospitality to outsiders, co-existence with members of hostile groups, joy instead of fasting (Mark 2.18f.), help instead of conformity to rules (Mark 3.1ff.), the demolition of prejudice (Matt. 7.2ff.) and above all a love which is extended even to enemies (Matt. 5.43ff.).

Like all religions, Christian faith corresponds to the appeal expressed by reality as a whole. However, its distinctive feature is that it sets a suffering man at the centre of religious experience, expressing the overwhelming absurdity of reality in the symbol of the cross and the wealth of its resonance in the notion of love. Christological symbolism makes us sensitive both to the negative side of our existence and to what enables us to resist it; to the experience of resonance in its manifold forms which finds its fulfilment in human love. But at this point an objection might arise. Is not the Christ event meant to be the revelation of God? Is it not meant to disclose God and make him accessible to man? Is that factor not ignored? In the context of the theory of religion, all symbols can be regarded as revelation which bring home to us the appeal contained in reality, which give us some inkling of its mystery and make it possible for us to shape our lives accordingly. Christological symbolism assures us that only through love can we do 'justice' to the whole of reality, for 'he who abides in love abides in God'.

However, christological symbolism is concerned not only to make us more sensitive but to put us under an obligation: to identify ourselves with the field of resonance in reality and to resist its absurdity. It is a protest against the experience of absurdity. The historical Jesus himself expressed a fourfold protest: against inhuman norms, social discrimination, the use of force and physical suffering. This protest recurs in christological poetry. For here the one who was judged becomes the judge of the world, the one who was discriminated against becomes the high priest, the underdog becomes the lord of the world, the sufferer becomes the source of life. The protest of the historical Jesus is symbolically heightened in christological poetry and as a result is raised above its character of accidental historicity. His protest is meant to apply universally, and not just in a particular historical situation.

Christological symbolism is a protest against the inhumanity of norms. Even with the historical Jesus we find an abolition of the law in favour of love. Legal norms are contrasted with spontaneous love which does not look for anything in return – either in the relationship between God and man, or in relationships between human beings. The time of legal treaties between God and man is past (Luke 16.16). Those with nothing to boast of are as acceptable as those who have made a great contribution (Mark 20.1ff.). Spontaneous help for others is not concerned with legal restrictions: the sabbath is made for man, not man for the sabbath (Mark 2.27f.). For the first time in history the insight dawns that cohumanity is more than morality and that morality can falsify cohumanity. The outline of a free covenant in love is set up over against relationships based on moral norms and laws. Furthermore, the ambivalence of moral norms is unmasked. Even with the historical Jesus we find a juxtaposition of the intensification of norms and the relaxation of norms. Demands are intensified to the utmost degree, e.g. erotic fascination for another woman is itself adultery (Matt. 5.27f.), while at the same time transgressors are accepted: the woman taken in adultery is not censured in any way (John 8.3ff.). The two things are closely connected: intensification of a norm demonstrates that no one can fulfil the norm. Thus anyone who is under the apprehension that he has fulfilled the norm and then discriminates against those who transgress it, through self-righteousness and hypocrisy transgresses against the greater commandment to show solidarity with his fellow-men. The symbolic actions of christological poetry make this changed attitude to the norm even clearer. The execution of the Son of God is a revelation of the aggressive and destructive power of the norm, an insight which has only been regained in modern times by Nietzsche and Freud: guilt feelings are aggression directed within. Since Paul's penetrating analyses we have become aware that the law kills. This is not just the Jewish law from Sinai; rather, a law is inescapably 'inscribed' on the hearts of all men (Rom. 2.14f.). Even Adam was faced with a command. Like every command, it promises a fuller life. It says: If you do this or that, you will attain to the true life.

But this promise is deceptive. It turns our energies in a false direction. For true life lies beyond the norm. Men attain to true life when their own life becomes a grateful response to the abundance of resonance in reality, which is already present without our doing anything about it. This is the one source of the demand to preserve and to further resonance. However, the law reverses this relationship. Its moral demands are like a barrier which increasingly separates us from the field of resonance in reality and makes us more and more incapable of accepting the meaning of our life as a gift. The law is unmasked in the symbolic actions of New Testament christology. It has condemned an innocent man. It has condemned the very man in whom the abundance of resonance in reality was present. In so doing, however, it has also shown its own helplessness. Christological poetry makes the condemned man the judge, who takes the place of the law that condemns – even in us: 'There is therefore now no condemnation for those who are in Christ Jesus' (Rom. 8.1). The aggressiveness of the internalized norm (psycho-analysts would say: the aggressiveness of the super-ego) is replaced by the spirit of Christ, of love and reconciliation. The judge who was once himself judged now acquits the guilty and makes possible a new beginning which, while not entirely without a norm, lacks the lethal aggressiveness of absolute norms. Thus the symbolic actions of New Testament christology bring about a radical change in our attitude to norm, law and morality. Anyone who allows the images of christological poetry to work on his unconscious will become free to accept himself and others without that distortion of resonance between human beings by guilt-feelings, projections and resentments to which norms give rise.

Christological symbolism is a protest against social discrimination. Human relationships are not just regulated by norms; to achieve stability here, withdrawal from outside groups often proves necessary. The greater the inner tensions that have to be overcome, the more pointedly particular outside groups have to be rejected, so that a stage comes when there are only friends and enemies, children of light and children of darkness (as in Qumran). By contrast, the historical Jesus teaches that solidarity should be shown not only towards those with whom we already have social connections but also towards others: outsiders, the despised, enemies. This identification with outsiders and the enemy appears again in the symbolic intensifications to be found in christological poetry: here Christ is made the scapegoat who bears the sins of the world. He becomes the radical outsider at whose expense a group seeks to establish its inner security. Normally the sacrifice is killed; the scapegoat has to go into the wilderness (Lev. 16), taking all tensions with him. In early Christianity, however, something truly revolutionary happened: the group did not drive its scapegoat away but identified itself with him; it bestowed supreme power on him, making the expiatory offering the sacrificing priest, the ruler of the world and the judge. The outsider became the central point of reference for the community. Those who went on to represent this sacrificial death in symbolic actions, to internalize these images of mythical fantasy, made a beginning in overcoming the scapegoat complex which burdens all relationships between human beings, even if no one can completely escape it. Is it not significant that those Christian groups which look for a realistic understanding of the dogma of the sacrificial death of Christ at the same time mourn the passing of the death penalty? Are they not like those Old Testament priests who, according to Hebrews 7.27, are compelled to keep offering bloody sacrifices for themselves? (It may be equally significant that many 'modern' theologians use virtuoso exegetical considerations to interpret away the sacrificial death of Christ.)

Christological symbolism is a protest against the use of force. Not that it is impossible to discover any use of force with the historical Jesus! Force is used in the 'cleansing of the Temple', to the degree of compelling people to leave the Temple forecourt. Jesus used force in a prophetic symbolic action – without physical harm, simply as a demonstration. This particular instance illuminates his attitude to force. For in him we find three elements of non-violent action which aim at changing an opponent's attitude: provocative infringement of regulations, as in the cleansing of the Temple or breaches of the sabbath; public criticism, e.g. of the rich and the pious; manifest defencelessness in accepting negative consequences, renouncing self-defence, in order to bring opponents to their senses.

Generally speaking, there were other successful non-violent actions against the Roman forces of occupation in Palestine at the time of Jesus. One such demonstration compelled Pilate to remove the imperial ensigns which he had smuggled into Jerusalem (Josephus, *Jewish War*, 2.174). Thus the argument that this is a strategy which can be carried out only by a private individual is historically false. Only in modern times, however, have the various elements in a non-violent resolution of conflict been developed into a systematic political strategy, by Gandhi and Martin Luther

King. In my view this is a decisive ethical step forward in the history of our culture, which in the last resort goes back to Jesus. In modern times, this strategy of non-violence is put at the service of social and political change; for Jesus it served the kingdom of God. However that concept may be interpreted, the coming of the kingdom of God resulted in the end of the Roman rule of Palestine. In contrast to other radical theocratic movements in his time, Jesus did not want to bring in the kingdom of God by force. But he did not wait for it inactively. The coming of the kingdom was indeed a miracle. But it also happened through miracles; and miracles could be performed (Matt. 12.28; 10.8). Charismatic non-violence, not passive inaction, was to overcome the imperial power. This feature recurs in the symbolic intensifications of christological poetry: the one who came to grief on the cross is appointed ruler of the world; the underdog who was executed by the political authorities becomes the one who holds all power in heaven and on earth. Because he humiliated himself, even to death on the cross, God exalted him above every power (Phil. 2.8f.). Here we have more than a change of authorities; we have a restructuring of power. Non-violence, which is physically inferior, is proclaimed as victor over all force. In the symbolic actions of primitive Christian christo- logy, man looks for the transcending of relationships based on force. All force, all power, will have to be judged by the way in which it deals with the powerless; and there is nothing less Christ- ian than the glorification of force or that slovenliness in dealing with it which can be found in our society (among governments, terrorists and a thoughtless public), no matter what the ideological premises to which particular states have subscribed. Christians are bound to a dream of a world without force; and it is just not true that we cannot get nearer to this dream.

Christological symbolism is a protest against physical suffering. The historical Jesus had more than normal capabilities and put them at the service of his cause. His miracles are a protest against deformity, sickness, hunger and death. For Jesus, those miracles were a sign of the dawn of the kingdom of God: 'But if it is by the Spirit of God that I cast out demons, then the kingdom of God has come upon you' (Matt. 12.28). Here Jesus distinguishes himself from those prophets who promise a wonderful future, but are pre- pared to sacrifice the present for the future. Happiness and help are to be found here and now: not only spiritual comfort, but physical help and healing. This feature, too, recurs in christological poetry. In it, the helpless sufferer who died on the cross becomes the source of a new life. On the basis of visions which are difficult to explain (but which cannot be dismissed as mere imagination), the disciples came to the conviction that he was risen; from then on they lived in the 'power of the resurrection' (Phil. 3.5), in which they took suffering and deprivation upon themselves. Here, too, the resurrection was not just something in the future. It already began in this life: 'Truly, truly I say to you, he who hears my word and believes him who sent me, has eternal life; he does not come into judgment, but has passed from death to life' (John 5.24). Certainly the hope of a future consummation was maintained. But the essential thing was that the future consummation was no longer purely future. It already began in the present. It began above all in those miraculous acts of help and salvation, in the renewal of life. Anyone who takes the imagery of christological poetry deeply to heart will not be content with dreaming of a better future in which physical suffering will be overcome: here and now he will seek ways of diminishing and overcoming suffering.

Christological symbolism is a heightening of the historical Jesus. It gives him universal significance over and above his historical situation. In addition to that it expresses something which could not be said with reference back to the historical Jesus. It interprets the life of Jesus as the incarnation of a deity, who after his death on the cross returned to heaven. As a result the status of being a man becomes a counterpoint to the status of being God, and the two are connected by the process of a radical change of status: in the imagery of christological poetry the condemned man becomes the judge who pronounces acquittal; the scapegoat becomes the sacrificial priest; the failure becomes the king who rules the world; the dying man becomes the source of life. Common to all these symbolic actions is the exchange of positions: the lowly one is exalted and the exalted one brought low. This produces a new definition of the experience of resonance: from now on, resonance is irrevocably a relationship without mastery, without force, without difference in status: from now on resonance is a brotherly attitude to people and things. Whatever is superior demonstrates its superiority by its power to empty itself. For the Son of God himself 'did not count equality with God a thing to be grasped, but emptied himself, taking the form of a servant' (Phil. 2.6f.). Whatever is humbled is destined to be exalted. For even the one who came to grief on the cross was exalted. He was 'obedient unto death, even death on a cross. Therefore God has highly exalted him' (Phil. 2.8f.). The abundance of resonance in reality is revealed in the humiliation of the exalted and the exaltation of the lowly. From this point on, the longing for resonance is no longer contradicted by that will to power which strives to subdue nature to man and man to his fellow man. True, it seems that lordship cannot be completely broken down. But the question remains: could it not be shaped in such a way that even the lowliest could be conceived of in the position of the highest and the highest in the position of the lowliest?

A decision for Christianity is a confession for christology, i.e. to carry out the symbolic actions of those primitive Christian groups by which they responded to the manifestation of the historical Jesus. Christology becomes revelation when as a result of it there is a new experience of the abundance of resonance and absurdity in reality – when despite subjective absurdity and objective meaning-lessness, despite sin and suffering, there is permanent access to the abundance of resonance in reality.

With the help of categories from the theory of religion we have attempted to explain why christology can still be accepted today. Without general criteria, such a confession would be irrational. However, the examination of the confession by means of general categories alters its character. When we are aware why we are accepting the central statements of the New Testament, we also become aware what has to be rejected. If the disclosure of reson-ance and revolt against absurdity become the decisive criteria, we have to reject those elements in the New Testament which limit resonance and love, e.g. all the beginnings of discrimination against other people on the grounds of ethical and religious meas-ures, no matter whether these are Gentiles, Jews, heretics, other believers, homosexuals or women.

4. Anthropological considerations

If we are concerned with a reasoned examination of the christolog-ical tradition; if we are stressing the inner truth of christo-logy and rejecting simple recourse to historical authority, do we not then find ourselves in conflict with the very tradition the truth of which we are attempting to demonstrate? Does not the New Testament bear manifest witness to an underivable act of God's revelation? Is not the New Testament proclamation clearly directed towards an ultimately underivable decision of faith? Yes, without a doubt. That is why we must return at the end of our discussion to the theology of the revealed decision which we attacked so strongly to begin with, and accept that it is justified. It has two sides: a divine side and a human side. The inexplicable revealed decision of God is matched by an equally inexplicable decision of human faith.

In my opinion, religious awareness is justified in returning to an underivable act of revelation. For what religions call 'revelations' are mutations of our general awareness which are as inexplicable and underivable as are the mutations of the genetic code within biological evolution. This comparison is meant to be more than an illustration. Behind it, rather, is the conviction that religious consciousness is subject to the same principles as the whole of evolution, indeed the whole development of our behaviour and knowledge. No matter what the aspect of biological and human development with which we are concerned, particular demands of the environment always lead to a variation in inherited or transmitted means of matching the demand, a variation which cannot be derived from the environment. It can consist in mutations and new combinations of the genetic code; it can consist in changes and new orderings of the traditional repertoire, of patterns of behaviour, in a revolutionary theory or a fundamental change in our religious attitudes. In this context the important thing is that even on the genetic level, the mutations arise unexpectedly and spontaneously. They are, however, stimulated by the pressure of selection from outside, even if they are not themselves 'explicable'. The majority of them do not give any guidance towards the future. On the contrary, just a few mutations lead to a productive new adaptation of life to its environment or to the conquest of new parts of the environment by life. The same is true of scientific theories, of ethical patterns of behaviour and of religious experiences. In each case they respond to a demand from the environment. But in the last resort they are inexplicable. All we can explain is why some of them win through and others do not. The origin of fundamental new beginnings in our cultural life is always somewhat 'irrational'.

Now a 'mutation' in our religious life consists in a new attitude towards reality and a new experience of it. 'Revelations' show us the whole of reality in a new light. They give us as it were a new organ for perceiving them, just as any progress in evolution gives us new organs for discovering the world. The light in which we look on the revelations of reality as a whole is, however, in the last resort the light of this reality itself – a light deriving from its most developed variants, which are as inexplicable and underivable as our existence itself. Here the mystery of reality meets us intensively and directly. We could say that here God encounters us. Thus there is some justification for a religious awareness which sees its origins from an inexplicable revelation. It corresponds to the situation. Once we recognize this, we do not renounce critical rationality, but apply critical rationality to a field which has all too long been overshadowed by that rationality.

Of course, what has come into being spontaneously and inexplicably is subject to critical examination – but this critical examination remains bound up with the spontaneous givenness of the insight and revelation to be examined. In the religious sphere this means that it remains bound to an event of proclamation. Arguments may help us to accept this proclamation, but in the last resort it is based on an act of faith. The element of decision in Christian faith should not, then, be disputed. But here, too, we can show why Christian faith necessarily has an element of decision in it, why it is bound up with a historical accident. Our argument is: because man is a finite being, i.e. because he suffers, goes wrong and is doomed to death, Christian truth remains bound up with a historical event of proclamation which can acquire unconditional significance for the individual.

The indissoluble connection between Christian truth and history lies in the fact that while we can make the conflict between resonance and absurdity generally clear, we cannot show why we should come down on the side of the field of resonance in reality, and why that should be the normative authority for our life – despite objective and subjective absurdity, despite sorrow and guilt. Does not our guilt prevent us from identifying ourselves with the field of resonance in reality? Who gives us the right to get beyond it? There are indeed rational grounds for supposing that it would be desirable for us not to be oppressed by guilt or sorrow. That is certainly more constructive; it has more positive consequences and is better for other people. But from what source do we obtain the right and the strength to realize the values we wish for? From what source do we derive the authority for declaring that separation from the field of resonance in reality is of no importance? Anyone who thinks that he can shake this off should be referred to Anselm of Canterbury: *Nondum considerasti quantum ponderis sit peccatum!* He is not yet aware of the magnitude of subjective (and objective) absurdity. Here now is a point where the Christian simply refers to Christ's conduct. Because Jesus has overcome this separation of sin and holiness, light and darkness, guilt and innocence, and accepted men, although they are unacceptable, it is also possible to overcome subjective absurdity. He is believed to have had the authority to forgive sins, an authority which was not removed even by his death; and one cannot give reasons for this confidence any more than for the confidence that despite all the absurdity, reality is to be affirmed. Courage to live in the face of sin and suffering is in the last resort based on an underivable act of faith. Faith is unconditioned motivation to live, for all its subjective and objective absurdity. Christian faith is that unconditioned courage to live which takes the figure of Christ as its point of reference.

Were man's capacity for fundamentally changing his life not limited, did he not have a restricted capacity for that new life which is depicted in the New Testament, he would not constantly need external stimuli: renewed appeals, proclamation, promise, rites. However, instead of living his life in response to the field of resonance in reality, man falls victim again and again to his natural egocentricity. Instead of being open to his fellow creatures, he keeps shutting himself in. Instead of allowing himself to be concerned with furthering love and understanding, he remains idle. So he is directed towards a community in which people remind one another of what man can all too easily betray. Were man perfect, then that prophecy from Jeremiah 31.34 would apply: 'And no longer shall each man teach his neighbour and each his brother, saying, "Know the Lord", for they shall all know me, from the least of them to the greatest, says the Lord; for I will forgive their iniquity and I will remember their sin no more.'

We tried to examine our confession of Christian truth on the basis of criteria from the theory of religion. However, anything that is tested by criteria cannot have absolute validity. Validity indeed means corresponding to criteria. But judgments made in this way can be corrected and revised. In turn, the criteria cannot make absolute claims: they are based on a critical reflection upon religious traditions and one's own experience. The use of criteria from the theory of religion can never lead to absolute validity. And if that is so, what can be valid absolutely? Does this denial of claims to absoluteness not bring us into conflict with the New Testament?

An objectively given tradition can never have unconditional validity; that can only apply to a tradition which is appropriated subjectively. For an unconditional nature we must look to a particular limited life which can never be brought back again. Everything of which we can speak, in which we delight and under which we suffer, for us (though not of itself) is bound up with the condition that we are alive. We in our turn can make our life dependent on conditions. We can sacrifice it for a cause; we can be so gripped by something that we cannot survive unless we do justice to it. Only reasons for giving up one's life have an unconditional character, though these reasons may appear historically relative and even questionable from another perspective. Nevertheless, they are unconditional reasons for the person risking his life. He can influence the consequences of all other decisions and retrospectively put the past decision in a new light by the way in which he behaves. But death knows no ifs and buts, no reservations, no corrections, no conditions under which it might be less fatal. It is irrevocable. It cannot be revised. The New Testament tradition only becomes unconditional once we have found in it something for which we are ready to die. The unconditional cannot therefore be demonstrated by arguments: it has to be lived out. It is the criterion of the martyrs and confessors. We do better to keep quiet about the 'unconditional' until we are prepared to apply this criterion. Anything less is thoughtless chatter.

However, inescapable death as well as voluntary death is an existential criterion for what we call the 'unconditional' and 'absolute'. Death is man's greatest challenge from the absurd. It is the hardest test of our yes to life, our identification with the field of resonance in reality. It threatens to hand over everything to absurdity. It leaves us nothing, absolutely nothing. Courage to live which stands fast in the face of death would be a *creatio ex nihilo,* creation from nothing, of the kind which is achieved in the symbolic actions of the resurrection. It would be groundless and contingent like everything else. And for that very reason, the contingency of all things would find a last echo in it. For in the last resort, death and transitoriness present us with the question whether we will affirm with all possible passion that something exists, and not nothing; whether we will affirm our life, even if there is no one alive thousands and millions of years hence who can affirm that it was meaningful; whether we identify ourselves with the field of resonance in such a way that we do not run away, though we may not be fighting on the side of the stronger battalions. That alone is unconditional affirmation, affirmation which makes no more conditions. Of course, the oppressive nature of a final farewell cannot diminish the fact that in our confrontation with death we are still aware that we belong in the field of resonance presented by reality and that the accent of eternity is placed on our life. Still, this can

97

diminish the poison of death's infection, so that we are capable of giving death no power over our thoughts because of goodness and love.[23]

Unconditional affirmation of life is the achievement of existential resonance; it is a response to the wonder of creation. For that reason it is not the legitimation of the absurd, which is still part of this creation. It is resistance against the absurd, and though our physical resistance may often be futile, we are still in the position of permanently refusing our assent to the absurdity of innocent suffering. We have the power never in any circumstances to assent to it. We have the power to reject its legitimacy, though that may be of supreme importance to traditional religion. This 'never in any circumstances' is a negative eternity; it is a form of eternity which can still be experienced indirectly when its positive elaborations fade away in the twilight of myth. The unconditional 'no' is the reverse of an unconditional 'yes', which man discovers like a great piece of good fortune when he is grasped by the field of resonance in reality and is raised above the grief of subjective absurdity. He then becomes aware that his transitory and vanishing life has infinite value as a response to the field of resonance in reality, even if it leaves hardly any traces behind and is characterized by transitoriness. He feels bound up with that mystery which he senses in all his experiences of resonances and absurdity, and which he calls God. He is surprised by the peace which is above all reason and towards which all the religions are moving.

It is now time to sum up our reflections on historical relativity. The Christian tradition is relative and historical through and through. However, in, with and under all historically relative traditions, symbols and images a truth is preserved which is valid for today. It is disclosed to those who are concerned with the fundamental religious problem of the conflict between resonance and absurdity, meaning and meaninglessness. This truth acquires unconditional binding force under the conditions of finite human existence. While the religious truth of Christian symbolism may be tested by arguments, it is an underivable act of faith to accord this truth unconditional power over one's own life.

And so we have come to the end of our journey. Our arguments in support of a critical faith were meant to establish which elements in Christian religion can stand the test if we take into account contemporary ideological, empirical and historical criticism. They began from a standpoint which was critical of religion. They sought out the truth of religion by following this criticism through, not countering it. They were born of the conviction that we must work such criticism out to the end if we are to show what elements in religion are valid and what are not. Anything else is an evasion. The way forward may have become clear. Outlines of a theory of religion have been developed in which religion has not only been described in phenomenological and historical terms, but has been explained from the relationship between man and the reality that surrounds him. This does not presuppose that religion has any timeless essence; it posits a historical process with continuity and discontinuity which is still far from being finished. In its course religion has changed profoundly and will continue to change. Certainly much has been omitted which might be expected of a theory of religion. I have limited myself to what I think important if I must defend my own belief. I hope that I have demonstrated sufficiently the difference between an approach made from the theory of religion and one based on the theology of the revealed decision. It is also clear that such an approach must seem a short cut to many people. For it deliberately leaves out of account what theology has largely claimed to be its special characteristic: the claim to privileged knowledge and an authority which is above human judgment. In this respect it openly acknowledges its 'spiritual poverty'. I am not interested in irrefutable assertions but in refutable truths. This question of the truth goes against much in life that is otherwise valuable. It causes resentment, at a time when agreement with others counts more than the correction of the errors of yesterday and today. It is not legitimated by faithfulness to the tradition, but shows its faithfulness to the tradition by being open to cross-examination. But it is open to argument, even to argument from dogmatic traditions. It allows itself to be irritated by arguments, for it is based on the recognition 'that I may be wrong and you may be right, and by an effort we may get nearer to the truth'.[24]

Notes

1. For the following analysis of the anthropological conditioning of religious experience I am much indebted to A. Gehlen, *Urmensch und Spätkultur,* Frankfurt 1964. A first outline of these notions was published in an excursus to my book *Urchristliche Wundergeschichten,* Gütersloh 1974, pp. 46–50.

2. S. Acquaviva, *Der Untergang des Heiligen in der industriellen Gesellschaft,* Essen 1964, pp. 33ff.

3. G. E. Lessing, 'Die Erziehung des Menschengeschlechts', in *Lessings Werke* III, ed. K. Wölfel, Frankfurt 1967.

4. M. Frisch, *Homo Faber,* Eyre Methuen 1957, p. 182.

5. For this see H. Thomas, *Das Individuum und seine Welt. Eine Persönlichkeitstheorie,* Göttingen 1968.

6. I am indebted to R. Kakuschke for this illustration.

7. For these distinctions see E. Topitsch, *Vom Ursprung und Ende der Metaphysik,* Vienna 1958. Id., 'Das mythologische Denken', in *Ideologie,* ed. K. Lenk, Neuwied 1961, pp. 92–102.

8. Albert Camus, *The Myth of Sisyphus,* Hamish Hamilton 1955, p. 29.

9. With this definition of religion I am taking up the work done in the philosophy of religion by Rudolf Otto, *The Idea of The Holy,* Oxford University Press 1950. It seems to me wrong that this approach has not been continued in the theology of the last fifty years.

10. Peter Berger, *A Rumour of Angels,* Allen Lane 1970.

11. Albert Einstein, *Ideas and Opinions,* Alvin Redman 1956, p.40.

12. Antony Flew, 'Theology and Falsification', in *New Essays in Philosophical Theology,* ed. Antony Flew and Alistair MacIntyre, SCM Press 1955, p. 96.

13. Werner Heinsenberg, *Physics and Beyond,* Allen and Unwin 1971, pp. 215f.

14. Albert Camus, *The Myth of Sisyphus,* p. 19.

15. J. W. Goethe, 'Elegie' (Marienbad Elegy), my translation. Full German text in Ronald Gray (ed.), *Poems of Goethe,* Cambridge University Press 1966, pp. 166–70.

16. Albert Schweitzer, *Strassburger Predigten über die Ehrfurcht vor dem Leben,* Gesammelte Werke V, Munich no date, pp. 117–34.

17. Albert Schweitzer, *My Life and Thought,* Allen and Unwin 1933, p. 186.

18. Thomas Mann, *Buddenbrooks,* Secker and Warburg 1930, p. 327.

19. J. W. Goethe, *Über Wahrheit und Wahrscheinlichkeit der Kunstwerke* (1798).

20. For investigation into motivation see H. Schiefele, *Lernmotivation und Motivlernen,* Munich 1974.

21. G. W. Allport, *Personality. A Psychological Interpretation,* Constable 1949.

22. For questions relating to the history of tradition see my works 'Wanderradikalismus', *Zeitschrift für Theologie und Kirche* 70, 1973, pp. 245–71, and *The First Followers of Jesus,* SCM Press 1978.

23. Thomas Mann, *The Magic Mountain,* Secker and Warburg [2]1945, p. 497.

24. K. Popper, *The Open Society and its Enemies,* Vol. II, Routledge and Kegan Paul [4]1962, p. 238.